PRAISE FOR *THE MUSIC BETWEEN US*

Music is the soundtrack of our lives. When you hear a song from your youth, it opens you to powerful remembrances. As Steve Litwer played guitar for dying people, offering them pleasure and comfort in their final days, his own early memories were activated. Through his journey he reveals to us how he found forgiveness and healing for his family and himself. This wonderfully written book is his story. Both funny and sad, it is at its heart a tale of compassion leading to personal healing, redemption, and joy.

—SAM LIEBOWITZ, THE CONSCIOUS CONSULTANT,
AUTHOR OF *EVERYDAY AWAKENING*

Volunteers with a range of talents and interests are important for the success of hospice care. In this book, Steve Litwer takes us with him on his journey as a volunteer bedside musician and introduces us to those very close to their final destinations. Meaningful encounters with these individuals inspired him to take a fresh look at his personal story of pain and ongoing inner battle, and helped him reach new levels of intimacy, empathy, compassion, and contentment.

—BETH BALLENGER, MSW, EXECUTIVE DIRECTOR,
ASCEND HOSPICE, MISSOURI AND KANSAS

As a hospice chaplain, I have been alongside Steve when lives became souls, souls became stories, and stories became sacred. Steve collected the best of these stories and shares them with us in The Music Between Us. I highly recommend the book and, more importantly, I cherish the gift of living music he so freely shares.

—CHAPLAIN CLARK H. SMITH, CROSSROADS HOSPICE

In music, a grace note is an embellishment that is not essential to the harmony or melody. In relationships, grace is the all-important and thoughtful goodwill we extend to others. The great secret of the musician who plays an instrument for a sick or dying person as Steve Litwer describes doing in his book The Music Between Us is the pure grace and redemption this gift gives back. As someone nears the end of life, the simple pleasure of listening to a favorite song or two and sharing memories of the past with a compassionate friend is humanizing. Music and connection are medicines that heal the soul.

—STEVEN G. EISENBERG, M.D., MEDICAL ONCOLOGIST,
AUTHOR OF LOVE IS THE STRONGEST MEDICINE

The Music Between Us is an authentic, powerful, and honest look at the journey we all take. Struggle, pain, and loss, but also joy, redemption, salvation, and bliss are always present in this improbable life. Each story in the book is compelling and Steve's personal journey is an awakening that inspires us and gives us hope.

—PAUL R. LIPTON, ATTORNEY AND AUTHOR OF
HOUR OF THE WOLF AND IN THESE FIVE BREATHS

Steve Litwer, a self-proclaimed bedside musician, has written a poignant reflection of his life as it was revealed to him through the memories and reflections of his hospice patients. As he ministered to his patients with compassion and care, each piece he offered on his guitar was a bridge of love between his heart and theirs. Did music bring him the peace he so fervently searched for, or was it the love that flowed through him, connecting to the ultimate sacred mystery of the dying soul? Perhaps both. This beautiful book brought me great joy as it celebrates the love that can fill music as it is offered to another.

—FLICKA RAHN, COMPOSER, SINGER, EDUCATOR, SOUND THERAPIST, AND AUTHOR OF *THE TRANSFORMATIONAL POWER OF SOUND AND MUSIC*

For Lisa,
By horse or other, its all
about the journey

The Music
Between Us

Memoir of a Bedside Musician

Steve Litwer
10/9/21

Steve Litwer

One Guitar Place
OVERLAND PARK, KANSAS

One Guitar Place/Steve Litwer
www.SteveLitwer.com
info@stevelitwer.com

Cover design by Gus Yoo
Author photo by Terrance L. Allen
Guitar doodle © Lorena Raven
Copy editing by Stephanie Gunning
Interior design © by Book Design Templates

Library of Congress Control Number 2020923152

One Guitar Place books are available at special discounts when purchased by libraries or in bulk for premiums and sales promotions as well as for fundraising or educational use. Special editions or book excerpts can also be created to specification. For details, contact the publisher at the address above.

The Music Between Us / Steve Litwer —1st ed.

ISBN 978-1-7355274-0-6 (paperback)

CONTENTS

For Cynthia, Stephanie, and Ariel.

And for my brothers, Mitch and Stu.

Music in the soul can be heard by the universe.

—LAO TZU

Popular music is the soundtrack of our individual lives.

—DICK CLARK

Imperfection is the prerequisite for grace. Light only gets in through the cracks.

—PHILIP YANCEY

Author's Note

Although the stories in this book are true, the names and identifying details of some of the individuals mentioned have been changed to protect their privacy.

Preface

After silence, that which comes nearest to
expressing the inexpressible is music.

—ALDOUS HUXLEY

Upon returning home from a business trip one evening, my wife, Cynthia, informed me that one of her close friends had called earlier that day. Marianne's husband, Dave, had suffered a heart attack. He was not expected to survive more than a few weeks and was quickly placed on hospice service. Marianne asked if I would bring my guitar and visit them in the care facility. I said I would.

At the hospice, I nervously entered Dave's room, not certain what to expect or if my presence would do him any good. I think Dave slept throughout my visit. It seemed to me that the main impact of my presence was on Marianne and the nurses and other hospice staff who wandered into his room that night, attracted by the sounds of my very soft, relaxing, fingerstyle acoustic guitar playing. The music was a respite for all of them.

I was deeply touched by my own response to the experience. I left Dave and Marianne after about an hour of music. Never had I been showed so much appreciation for just showing up. Dave lived about another week.

This was a few years before my retirement. I was fifty-four.

Prior to this experience, I had never spent time with a dying person, not even my parents, who had lived across the country from me and whose deaths were relatively sudden. Certainly, the idea of playing music for someone at the end of life would never have occurred to me if Marianne hadn't made her request.

Years later, I learned there are people who do what I did that night—but not many. These musicians are usually volunteers, both professionals and amateurs, like me, who regularly visit sick or dying folks and try to brighten their spirits. Informally, we are known as *bedside musicians.*

Eleven years later, I would be retired, spending hours a day entertaining myself with my guitar, spending time with grandchildren and doing a bit of volunteer work for my church. It was a splendid existence. I was quite content with who I was and what I had achieved in my professional life. And then I found an email in my inbox. It was a newsletter that posted openings for volunteers at nonprofit organizations. I had signed up to receive it soon after retiring, hoping to find some type of meaningful part-time service work I could engage in.

The first posting was for an area hospice. The notice read:

Be a hospice volunteer. Volunteers give their time and compassion to patients and families dealing with end-of-life care needs. We rely on our volunteers to assist us in delivering exceptional care. Listed below are a few special service areas where volunteers are particularly needed:

- Volunteers with trained pet therapy animals.
- Musicians who can play for patients in their homes or in facilities.
- Bereavement volunteers to spend time with families after a death.

- Special services volunteers, such as beauticians and massage therapists.
- Volunteers who can play games or read to patients.

After reading this message, I knew playing for dying individuals would be an activity I would explore. By the end of that week, I had interviewed with the administrators, submitted to a background check, and gone through the required training for hospice volunteers. I was told that when called upon I would play music in private performances in a patient's room at a healthcare facility or in their home. My simple role would be to provide a comforting presence and play music that matched their mood and musical tastes in order to comfort them. I would be called a few days prior to my weekly assignments and given the details: The patient's name, age, diagnosis, and anything else about them that might be helpful to my visit, like whether they were married, had children, or had special interests.

Over three years and 300 musical visits later, what started as a nice little daily retirement diversion had evolved into something more and unexpected. Along the way, I stopped thinking of the individuals I visited as patients. I began seeing each one more deeply, with the potential for a genuine human connection that every new relationship offers. Thus, patients became clients. Mine would not be a medical role or part of a defined treatment plan that might yield a measurable health outcome. Rather, as with any relationship, each encounter would be something of an improvisation in which I am sharing the gifts of my time and my music with no expectation beyond the listener's satisfaction. The unexpected outcome would be this book.

The Music Between Us at its heart is as much a journal of self-discovery as it is a memoir of my experiences in playing music for people in hospice and reflecting on my own life while doing so. It's about a man slowly healing old wounds, spurred on by his time spent with those who cannot heal, and about the mysterious way God presented him an opportunity to understand and reclaim his life through the sharing of music with those who did not have much life left.

Most major faith traditions call for us to love the stranger. A logical extension of this guidance is to love and care for those most vulnerable. While not all dying folks are helpless, none can remedy his or her condition. This story reveals a bit of the mystery that can take place between two people who may be bound by nothing more than a melody offered without asking for anything in return. These moments of connection made possible through song have helped me to find my voice and discover my own story. As it turns out, I too am the vulnerable stranger.

Truly, music is medicine for the soul.

Introduction

Music gives a soul to the universe, wings to the mind,
flight to the imagination, and life to everything.

—UNKNOWN

I've never supported myself by teaching or performing music. I was simply not gifted enough to pursue a career in music. Thus, my professional life led me in another direction: a career in advertising. Fortunately, soon after retirement I discovered there was a captive audience waiting to enjoy my modest musical talents. These are people nearing the end of their lives. In short, they are terminally ill, dying either at home or in a healthcare facility. I am blessed to be with these individuals every week, playing music that might ease their journey.

Grounded in extensive neuroscience research, it is well known that music can tap deep emotional recall, even for patients with severe dementia. For example, for individuals afflicted with Alzheimer's disease, recent memories of common things like names and places and recollection of how to do everyday tasks is compromised, whereas recall of a life experience from childhood, adolescence, or young adulthood can be quickly triggered by the melody or lyrics to a song associated with an event.

Many scientific studies have explored how our brains respond to music. However, not every person with dementia responds in a predictable manner. The minds of some with advanced dementia are so far gone that they don't remember their own names. Those with other conditions may be so close to life's end that they are unable to engage with the music in an observable way. For these folks, I pray that the music I play is providing subtle benefits. Other times, I have seen someone:

- Who has been silent or barely communicative begin to talk or sing.
- Who has been sad or depressed smile and exhibit upbeat behavior.
- Who has shown little physical movement sit up, tap their feet, or display other body movements, keeping in time with the music.
- Share a thought on what the next step in their journey might look like.
- Show curiosity about my life and offer advice.
- Inspired by the music or our conversation reveal surprising life stories about their relationships, achievements, and adventures and how they feel about them.

The sharing of music is much like the sharing of stories. I think we tell each other stories to express ourselves and know we are not alone. Somehow, our listeners' confirmation lets us know that whatever we are sharing is understood and meaningful. If they can relate to the story, they are relating to us as people at some level. Likewise, in the hearing of stories, we know we are not alone. In both the telling and listening, we are often able to make sense of our own experiences through a two-way lens with another.

Music is much the same way. The sharing of music seems to dissolve the artificial barriers that separate people. Total strangers are easily joined together when relating to a song or a certain style of music. Yet, music may go a step further, conjuring the most enticing or painful memories of our lives: loves won and lost, successes and disappointments, family and friends. Certain songs take us back, reminding us of where we were at certain times in our lives and how we felt. However, they may also open painful doors we haven't walked through in a very long time—murky pieces of our past, hidden from us. These may be buried but are never gone. Even unfamiliar songs, depending on their musical style, can stir up feelings and specific memories.

In short, everyone has a story. I have heard many tales recounted while playing guitar as a bedside musician or streaming music from a commercial music service on my phone for people in hospice. At times, pieces of my own history will emerge as a result of sharing music and listening to those who still can communicate verbally near the end of their lives. As we talk during a musical visit, I find that many are very interested in hearing about me.

Over the years since I became a volunteer, I've come to realize that while I'm there to provide relief, pleasure, and amusement, I am also receiving these same gifts and much more from my listeners. Somewhere in the midst of our shared exchanges, both spoken and unspoken, my past history has become intertwined with my present, each informing the other. Many feelings and memories that I had hidden from others and myself have resurfaced, some the result of interactions with specific clients, but mostly from the cumulative effect of time spent with so many other humans, each of whom had the story of a full life.

Gradually, gently, this has led me to recapturing my own story, and with it, greater self-acceptance and peace.

How Bedside Music Performances Differ from Clinical Music Therapy

Bedside music performances are not part of a music therapy program. They can be therapeutic but are not therapy in a clinical sense. Clinical music therapy is an established health profession in which music is used within the context of a therapeutic relationship to address specific physical, cognitive, and emotional needs of individuals. Practiced by credentialed professionals, music therapists typically have a degree in the field that requires knowledge of psychology, medicine, and music.

Music therapists develop ongoing treatment plans for specific health conditions with specific and measurable outcomes in mind.

Bedside musicians do not seek to cure a health condition or illness. The goal of their performances is to allow music to comfort patients and family members. This comfort may include alleviating isolation, loneliness, and boredom. This non-clinical approach to the sharing of music can make each bedside performance a unique and spontaneous event for both the musician and the patient.

1 The Oldest Rock and Roll Groupie

BOUDLEAUX BRYANT, "ALL I HAVE TO DO IS DREAM," 1958,
PERFORMED BY THE EVERLY BROTHERS

Name: Liza

Age: 80

Diagnosis: Acute respiratory failure and dementia

For some clients, music triggers long-forgotten memories and emotions that haven't been observed previously by regular caregivers. Many studies have shown that music engages broad neural networks in the brain, including the brain regions responsible for motor actions, emotions, and creativity.

For example, one hub that music activates is located in the medial prefrontal cortex region—right behind the forehead—which, coincidentally, is one of the last areas of the brain to atrophy over the course of Alzheimer's disease. Even so, one doesn't really know when music, or which type of music, might evoke a response.

I don't think about any of this when I play music for someone. I merely try to bring a smile and some joy to their existence with songs I think a patient might enjoy. At one nursing home, about twenty minutes into my performance, I said I was going to play a couple of Everly Brothers songs. As I began the first song, my listener, Liza, loudly called out, "DONNIE!"

Here's the conversation that ensued.

Me: Donnie?

Liza: Yeah, Donnie!

Me: Who's Donnie?

Her: Donnie Everly.

Me: You mean Don Everly of the Everly Brothers?

Her: Yes, we dated.

Me. Really? (Said skeptically.) When was this?

Her: When I was fourteen.

Me: Who else was in the Everly Brothers (I was testing her.)

Her: Don't you know? Phil. I knew their dad too, Ike Everly.

Me: Where was this?

Her: Shenandoah, Iowa, where they lived.

Me: Where did you live?

Her: In Glenwood, Iowa.

Me: If you were just fourteen years old, how'd you get from Glenwood to Shenandoah?

Her: I hitchhiked.

Me: Were Don and Phil Everly famous at that time?

Her: Oh no, this was a few years earlier. . . . We were just kids.

This line of questioning went on for a while. I figured she knew just enough to spin a nice little story and probably made up a few facts too. (She insisted that she'd visit Donnie every week and they'd practice yodeling together!) When I jokingly asked for her autograph, she adamantly said, "I'm almost eighty and don't do autographs!" It was very comical how matter of fact her answers were.

Of course, I wasn't sure about any of it. However, I was curious. When I got home, I went online to check her story. As it turns out, the Everly Brothers had in fact lived in Shenandoah,

Iowa. I then mapped the distance to her hometown. There is a Glenwood, Iowa, and it's just thirty-eight miles from Shenandoah. The Everly Brothers' dad was in fact named Ike. Finally, I did the math, working the years backward. She was probably born around 1938, making her fourteen in 1952, just a year younger than Don Everly (born in 1937). Four years later, the Everly Brothers recorded their first professional record.

Liza was one of my earliest discoveries of how deeply a person's emotions and memories can be triggered through the hearing of music. Prompted by our conversation, these memories got very specific and resulted in recapturing the fondness she had experienced as a young girl in a relationship.

It didn't escape me that the year Liza began seeing Don Everly was the year I was born. Due to my online investigation, I rediscovered how many of the Everly Brothers songs (for example, "Cathy's Clown," "Bye Bye Love," and "Crying in the Rain") were dominating the radio airwaves at about the time I received my first guitar as a boy. I guess both of our neural networks were really lit up by the music and memories. My own personal exploration was about to begin.

The memories with which I struggle are those of my childhood with a sick mother. At age thirty-six, she was diagnosed with both paranoid schizophrenia and bipolar disorder, the latter condition known at the time as manic depression. I was fifteen. This was after years of exhibiting the slowly emerging behaviors associated with these disorders. Being raised by someone who suffers from these conditions leaves emotional scars that are nearly impossible to completely erase because many are so deeply buried. Moreover, because the behaviors of a parent are often adopted unknowingly by the child, one raised by a mentally ill person may learn to see the world in ways that are distorted, similar to how the parent perceives the world. In the case of children of schizophrenics, many of us grow up with intense feelings of guilt, shame, and worthlessness due to our experience. There is a nagging feeling of defectiveness and being found out.

When my mom's sickness really began to surface prominently, I was about thirteen. I have two brothers, Mitch and Stu, who at that time were eight and four. All of us were too young to understand what was going on with her. Growing up, we adapted in our own ways to living with someone whose occasional odd behaviors slowly evolved into full-scale delusions and hallucinations. These manifested as deeply held irrational fears and the breakdown of ordinary life skills. Our parents had divorced that year, probably because of my mother's paranoia, her inability to maintain relationships and my dad's inability to cope with it all. My father was rarely emotionally present to provide a calming balance and protect us from her.

From my thirteenth birthday on, my mom experienced classic schizophrenic and bipolar symptoms, which grew more frequent and severe: extreme depression, disorganized speech, inability to connect emotionally with herself and others, and antisocial behavior. These were accompanied by a breakdown in the functioning of common everyday activities like personal hygiene, housekeeping, and cooking. Of course, it was nearly impossible for her to get or keep a job given the strange behaviors that employers saw immediately, ones that we as children experienced as normal.

My mother's disintegration happened very gradually, commencing long before my teen years. My first memory of her acting "scary" was when I was about age four. She'd mysteriously faint after getting angry with me, which seemed to be often and for no discernible reason. By my thirteenth year, the most disconcerting behaviors were hallucinations. These would manifest as voices she heard in her head with whom she would have actual screaming arguments as I stood by listening and watching, not understanding what was happening or at whom she was screaming.

Mom also experienced unexplainable delusions. For example, she had a fear of anyone or anything Irish. Thus, we boys were forbidden to play with the neighbors who lived across the street from our home. They were Irish by descent. The mere mention of names like Murphy, Kelly, or O'Brien would be the start of hysterics. I once found a four-leaf clover in our yard. When I showed it to her, she went crazy, screaming at me.

Then, there was her anger with the government. During my teens I'd hear her on the phone on a regular basis, trying to reach the attorney general of the United States. When that failed, she decided that she must speak with the president himself. She believed the feds owed her millions of dollars they were withholding. I remember wondering about the response of the individuals at the other end of the line as she yelled obscenities and demands for payment.

As with many who suffer from mental illness, my mother had no friends. As a result of her paranoid delusions and odd behaviors she also alienated everyone in her extended family, all of whom she believed were in some way responsible for her problems or else not providing support she believed they owed her. Thus, over a period of years, as her symptoms became more frequent and pronounced, we had less and less contact with our grandparents, aunts, uncles, and cousins. As she became weirder and weirder, her older brother and sister and their families, who used to be a part of our lives and with whom we'd formerly shared occasional weekend visits, vacations, and holiday gatherings, disappeared.

By the time I turned thirteen, when my parents divorced, me and my siblings had seen most of these relatives for the last time. My brothers and I were never again invited to their homes. I suppose they didn't want to deal with our mom, as she had rejected the little help they could offer. There would be no white knights to rescue us; the cavalry would never arrive.

Years later, my relatives would tell each other that they offered to be supportive if she'd agree to get help. It was a hollow offer. She had become incapable of accepting assistance from people who had become a part of her delusions. Negotiating with a person suffering from schizophrenia is not often a fruitful endeavor. So, they simply carried on with their own lives.

When I was sixteen, our mom was involuntarily committed to Belleville Hospital in New Jersey, the first of many such interventions. I don't know who had the idea to get her help, but I was relieved. She was there for about two weeks. This was also the hospital where some of the movie *A Beautiful Mind* was filmed. That film is the story of legendary Nobel Prize-winning mathematician and schizophrenic John Nash, played by actor Russell Crowe. Due to his high intellect and analytical mind, he developed the very rare ability to recognize his hallucinations and delusions and determine if they were real or just symptom of his disorder.

When Mom returned home, she was more rational and much calmer due to the medication she had been prescribed. However, without ongoing psychotherapy, and as a result of her refusal to continue taking her meds, it didn't last.

By the time I reached my mid-teens, in order to cope, I developed survival mechanisms. The only healthy one was an immersion into music. I began spending much of my time playing guitar at the homes of friends who were also musicians.

2 The Woman Who Wasn't Looking for a Husband

ALEX NORTH AND HY ZARET, "UNCHAINED MELODY," 1955,
PERFORMED BY THE RIGHTEOUS BROTHERS

Name: Harriet
Age: 84
Diagnosis: Stroke

In advance of some musical visits, I imagine playlists of possible songs to play. At times it can be hard to know precisely what will appeal to a client if they are unable to tell you. A variety of factors inform my choices, like the stage of their condition and their mood when I arrive to perform. Regardless, a starting point is usually their age. For many, their favorite songs often date back to their youth.

This is also true for most of us. These songs are the easiest to remember and seem to provide the most joy. Searching online for research on this phenomenon, I ran across something called the *lifespan retrieval curve.* This is a graph that represents the number of autobiographical memories stored in the brain at various ages during one's lifespan. Lots of studies reveal roughly three stages of memory retrieval for most people. From birth to five years old is a time of amnesia. Age fifteen to around twenty-five the reminiscence bump, with a surge in recollection. Then, the mid-twenties to the present is the phase of forgetting. This appears to be a universal biological reality of the human brain.

Regarding the reminiscence bump, it's not just music that's easiest to recall. Also, specific movies and TV shows, books, and even radio and TV commercials. Memories of emotionally charged experiences and their attendant feelings may also be heightened.

Harriet was one of my early musical visits. Counting back from her current age, an eighty-four-year-old was twenty in 1955. That would have placed her in the reminiscence bump. That period also happened to be the dawn of the rock and roll era. Thus, playing a medley of mid to late 1950's love ballads might evoke some terrific feelings. My wife had recently suggested that I learn "Unchained Melody," the beautiful, well-known hit sung by the Righteous Brothers. It would surely be a winner with clients of Harriet's age.

Proud of my analysis, in plotting my visit with Harriet I decided I would perform a medley from that era. "Unchained Melody" would be the first of four songs. Harriet, who had been sitting quietly in her wheelchair, just staring at the floor, suddenly looked up, interrupted the music, and in the sternest tone, said, "I ain't lookin' for a husband!"

Not understanding the reason that she said this, I glibly stated, "Me neither, I'm married!" I then went on to play the next two songs in my medley, Elvis Presley's "Can't Help Falling in Love" and "Love Me Tender."

Before I finished the second tune, Harriet gave me a dirty look and said, "I thought I told you, 'I ain't lookin' for no husband!' Why don't you go play for some of the other ladies around here?" Finally, I asked her if she really wanted me to leave, and she said yes . . . that I should go find some other ladies who might be "interested."

It's difficult to know a patient's frame of mind and predict how they'll respond to the music or to our conversation. Unpredictably, Harriet thought I was serenading her and took it to heart. She found it disturbing. Was her response the result of her condition? It occurred to me there might also have been negative psychological and environmental factors at play during her reminiscence bump stage.

After that visit, I began asking clients or family members for the names of their favorite songs, artists, and musical styles. If I don't know them on the guitar, I'll stream them on my phone.

I was so unnerved, I stopped playing "Unchained Melody."

The idea of the reminiscence bump and musical memory association triggered by my visits left a lasting impression on me. As my number of clients expanded, so did some of my own most vivid childhood recollections.

I received my first guitar at age eight, when our family was living in Queens, New York. Purchased by my dad, it was a small acoustic guitar, a surprise gift. I don't recall it being my birthday or any other special occasion. Neither of my parents had any musical talent. I loved that instrument. Though, like lots of kids, I was not disciplined at practicing my weekly music lessons. It was slow going at first, but that guitar and I got close. I kept it in my bedroom closet, right next to my bed, and played it often since there was not much else going on in my life.

As for my mother, some of the symptoms of schizophrenia and bipolar disorder that emerged just a few years later were already present albeit muted. She would vacillate from being suddenly exuberant and affectionate to being sullen and withdrawn and commonly overreacting to the slightest inconveniences of daily life. This would be a behavior I learned from her when I encountered life's unexpected minor curveballs, both as a kid and an adult. She also had frequent fainting spells.

At some point, very early in my life, the strange behaviors of my mother became personal and abusive, years before anyone knew with certainty that she was ill. Unfortunately, nobody realized this soon enough to alter my lifelong patterns of responding with confusion or anger to any perceived irrational behavior on the part of others, especially women.

At around age four: After one of her fainting spells, Mom told me to go over to the phone and call my father who was at work. I told her I didn't know how. She told me the numbers, but I hadn't yet learned numbers and thus couldn't figure out where they were on the phone. Growing increasingly frustrated, she yelled at me. I felt dejected and stupid.

At age five: She tried to teach me to spell my name: Pen in hand, she wrote: **S t e v e n.** Handing me the pen, she left the room, telling me to practice the first letter of my name. Upon her return, I proudly demonstrated my letter "S."

ƨ ƨ ƨ ƨ ƨ

Seeing I had inverted the letter, she impatiently showed me once again and handed me back the pen and paper. I then carefully tried to copy what she had written:

ƨ ƨ ƨ ƨ ƨ

We went back and forth a few more like this with no change in my letter "S" formation. Finally, she lost her temper, screaming at me to pay attention, and then slapped me hard across the face.

At around age six: My mother tried to teach me how to tie my shoelaces. The outcome was not good for me.

At age seven: One Sunday, which also happened to be Mother's Day, I attended a movie matinee in my neighborhood. My parents never went to see movies with me. So, as usual, I sat alone in the theater. I don't recall the movie. I do remember finding a tube of used red lipstick under the seat directly in front of me. Having no money and no knowledge of how to buy things, I was very excited with my idea to present it to my mom when I returned home, as a Mother's Day present. Upon taking it from me, she threw it in the trash and sent me to my room for giving her such a filthy thing—but not before telling me that she wished I had never been born. I would hear that line many times while growing up.

Any one of these episodes might be dismissed as one-off unexplainable incidents in the life of any child, some remembered and others not, on the way to adulthood. However, their cumulative impact and increasing frequency traumatized me at a very early age.

I don't recall at what point anyone in our family realized Mom was sick. My two younger brothers vaguely recall always knowing something was wrong with her. Being five and nine years younger, her symptoms were already full-blown when they were little. For me, her dysfunctions appeared so gradually that I didn't notice until her symptoms crossed a significant threshold. I had become accustomed to her oddities, not knowing how deformed they were making me.

My dad must have been too emotionally unaware to sense signs of mental illness in her. Or just too weak to address the situation even once he finally became aware that something was very wrong. Before their divorce, when things got crazy, he usually just left the house, leaving us kids there with her. Looking back, I now realize it was an escape from having to deal with our environment. Even up until his death, he strangely never initiated a single conversation about our mother's illness or what it must have been like for all of us. When we quizzed him about it as adults, he usually had little to say. On one occasion I cornered him for an answer. He simply said, "It was so bad, I can't remember."

By age nine, I had blocked out most experiences that included my parents. At my young age, Mom's strange behavior had become normal, even if it often left me with a knot in my stomach. It's what I had gotten used to. I don't know exactly when it began, but I can remember distinctly thinking for the first time that I didn't like her. She acted weird and would yell or punish me for the slightest perceived misbehavior. I grew to learn that any minor misbehavior might result in being beaten with the buckle end of a belt.

Around 1962, when I was almost ten years old, we had moved from New York City to Edison, New Jersey, a suburban bedroom community, around forty miles southwest of Manhattan. My father had taken a new job. That's about the time our family's social isolation slowly began. My parent's interactive skills were apparently not well developed. I guess other folks sensed my mother's slightly odd behaviors. Few people came to visit us at home and our family didn't seem to be invited anywhere either, not even at the neighbors. Mom didn't work and was too nervous to learn to drive. Thus, when my dad was at work, we had no way to go anywhere.

This was quite challenging since we lived in a typical suburban community where there was virtually no mass transit. If we had to get someplace, we did it on foot. I can recall walking with my mother to the grocery store with an empty pushcart and making the same journey back home with the cart filled with grocery bags—probably a two-mile roundtrip hike.

Although my memories of childhood were few when I began volunteering, their emergence accelerated when I began spending time several days a week with hospice clients. Among the most prominent are my memories of music, which was my lifeline. As a kid, I had periods of daily pleasure listening to our tabletop kitchen radio when my mom wasn't in the room. When there, she'd usually turn it off without explanation. Most music annoyed her.

Some of my favorite songs from that period are:

- "Walk Right In," The Rooftop Singers
- "Alley Oop," The Hollywood Argyles
- "Itsy Bitsy Teenie Weenie Yellow Polka Dot Bikini," Brian Hyland
- "Walk Don't Run," The Ventures
- "Sleep Walk," Santo and Johnny Farina
- "Teen Angel," Mark Dinning
- "The Twist," Chubby Checker
- "Runaway," Del Shannon
- "Michael, Row the Boat Ashore," Peter, Paul and Mary

Although I recall few details from childhood, I do remember the day I got that first guitar. It was a kid-sized acoustic model with a tobacco sunburst finish. Made by the Harmony Guitar Company, I think it was purchased at JCPenney. It was a cheap model and awfully hard to play. My little fingers always hurt while strumming and picking. I did, however, learn the easier parts of two of my favorite songs, "Walk Right In" and "Michael, Row the Boat Ashore." My playing was terrible, but this was the first time in my life I can recall feeling like I was mastering something.

3 The After Beats

Music is an outburst of the soul.

—Frederick Delius

Name: Claire
Age: 98
Diagnosis: Peripheral vein disease

One afternoon, I visited a patient who lived in a small apartment in an assisted living facility. Often with a person of Claire's age, I expect to see lots of photographs of adult children, grandchildren, and great-grandchildren as well as old books and personal memorabilia reflecting an era long before my time. I usually carry a concern that the songs in my repertoire may be too recent and thus unrecognizable. Her musical reminiscence bump would likely be music of the 1930s and 1940s.

Claire's daughter, Karen, let me in when I arrived. She looked to be in her mid-sixties. Her mother had been getting dressed in another room. As we talked, I found a good place to sit myself. I also took out my phone and set up a small wireless speaker, figuring I'd be streaming most of the songs her mom might recognize. When Claire rolled into the den in her wheelchair, she was bright-eyed and smiling. Her hair was partially braided, and she wore a bright shade of red lipstick. On her left hand were leather bands, each strung with turquoise stones separated by silver objects. She had made these herself.

After we introduced ourselves, I asked what kind of music Claire enjoyed. She pointed to a small, framed tabletop photo of five teenage boys. That picture looked to be a promotional photo. Shot in black and white, the teens were posing in iridescent suits with skinny black ties. Each had an instrument in their hands. The one kid that got my attention was holding a bass guitar built by Hofner Guitars, the same model used by Paul McCartney when the Beatles first burst onto the American music scene. The haircuts in the photo gave away the time period: around 1964 or 1965. I knew all this because those years had gripped me when I was a preteen.

I asked Claire who the kids were. She said they were the After Beats, a Kansas City version of bands like the Beatles and other British rock groups of that era, like the Kinks, the Animals, the Dave Clark Five, and Gerry and the Pacemakers.

Karen was watching my expression of surprise that her mother had even been aware of that piece of rock and roll history. She smiled and said that one of the boys in the picture was her brother. Her mom then said, "Play something like they did." Suddenly I flashed back to the music from the period in that photo. I played "Walk Right In," one of the earliest songs I had learned to play.

Mistakes and all, Claire immediately recognized the song and gave me the biggest smile of recognition. I then played three early Beatles songs: "If I Fell," "In My Life," and "Kansas City." It seems her son's music infatuation ran parallel to mine. As a young musician roughly the same age, I too had gotten caught up in the excitement of the British Invasion.

Our visit seemed to ignite Claire's memory of her son's brush with local fame over fifty years earlier.

Before I left, the three of us told some stories. I shared that during the summer of 1965 I attended my first-ever rock concert on the Steel Pier in Atlantic City, New Jersey. The band was Herman's Hermits. I don't remember a single thing about that performance except the girl I met at that show. Her name was Heidi. I was thirteen, she twelve. After the concert, we walked on the boardwalk and sat down on a bench overlooking the beach. I recalled nervously placing my arm around her shoulder, feeling the softness of her blue mohair sweater, and sharing a brief kiss—my first-ever of those too.

Shortly after the visit with Claire and her daughter, my hospice liaison told me that Claire's son had committed suicide in his twenties. I was stunned by the likely blending of sadness and joy in Claire at briefly reexperiencing and discussing the musical triumphs of her son. Perhaps the music had become the marker for her fondest memories of him, a perfect snapshot made possible by the healing power of the years.

Very few individual visits with clients have provided me with jolts of memories of specific people, places, and events from my past. My slow discovery of memories is more the overall accumulated effect of spending time with hundreds of clients. As I have learned to allow others to be vulnerable with me, letting them feel safe in their expression, my own vulnerabilities and hidden memories have come floating to the surface more easily and feel less threatening. One of the few visits that did actually trigger actual memories was the one with Claire and her daughter.

When I was twelve in 1964, like just about everyone I knew, I encountered the musical tsunami known as the Beatles. Liberated from the pop music styles of the late 1950s and early

1960s, with the so-called British Invasion we baby boomers suddenly got a refreshing dose of a new musical and cultural reality. The band's popularity led to dramatic changes in hairstyles, fashion, and a sort of bending of the culture. An irreverent, unorthodox way of looking at the world was emerging that was a radical departure from anything our parents had known.

For teens, the 1960s arrived on a wave of new sounds. My thirteenth year would be marked by other life-altering events. My cheap acoustic guitar was replaced by a cheap electric guitar and an amplifier purchased with money I earned delivering daily newspapers in our neighborhood on my bike. I was determined to be a rock and roll star. That was my all-consuming fantasy. When I was alone in my room, I pretended to be on a stage playing my greatest hits. That year was also the year my parents divorced.

At home things had been deteriorating. I can recall sitting on the front stoop of our suburban home, contemplating the divorce, relieved that I would no longer have to hear my parents' nightly battles, which had gotten physical. I vividly recall one episode of my dad dragging my hysterical mom through our home by her hair, pulling her across the floor to the bathroom and forcing her into the shower to calm her down. I sat in my bedroom quietly watching. I felt nervous and afraid and quickly blocked out the memory of the violence. Over fifty years later, something about my musical visit with Claire resurfaced not just the episode, but my feelings about it. Suddenly I was thirteen again, watching my world implode.

It was also around this time that our father lost his job after being accused of embezzling money at the company where he worked as an accountant. I didn't know exactly what that meant, but the word *embezzler* sounded ominous. Was he stealing money from the company safe? Would he go to jail? This did not seem like a good thing. My unemployable mother had gone crazy over the insecurity of us having no income and no savings.

I realized years later that, as an accountant, Dad probably had more clever methods of stealing. Yet, employed or not, with my dad no longer living with us, a cloud lifted.

As an adult, I slowly recognized that Dad had lots of emotional issues of his own. After all, what kind of person has a fifteen-year marriage to a person like my mom and has no inkling that she might be mentally ill? How was he even initially drawn to her? When these thoughts first entered my mind, I quickly put them aside because a life with two off-kilter parents was unthinkable. At least he wasn't bat-shit crazy like her.

Just prior to the divorce, when I was twelve, Dad lost his driver's license because he found himself in a car accident without insurance. His license had been revoked but not his car, and he chose to drive anyway. Because he was such a lousy driver, he was continuously being pulled over by the police. Of course, he was busted each time for not having a valid license, and, each time, he was fined, and the driving revocation was extended further into the future.

Five years later, during the summer after my high school graduation, my dad was allowed to reapply for licensure and take the required driving test. This exam included a short drive through an obstacle course with an officer in the front passenger seat. I will never forget being in the back seat and thinking that once he earned back his license, he could teach me to drive. All my friends were already driving. Since neither of my parents could drive legally and my dad's car was parked somewhere most of the time, this was a very big deal. As I've said, my brothers and I basically had grown up walking everywhere or begging people for rides.

Dad flunked the test that day for speeding through the obstacle course and not being able to parallel park. I left for college a month later, flying to Chicago's O'Hare Airport. From there, I hitchhiked to the tiny town of Milton, Wisconsin, and began my freshman year of college. It took him another couple of years to get back his license. All in all, he had been without a valid license for around seven years.

4 Meatballs with a Side of Music

Music is the shorthand of emotion.

—Author Unknown

Name: John
Age: 83
Diagnosis: Senile degeneration of the brain

The atmosphere within healthcare facilities, like assisted living and nursing communities, is obviously different from that of a private home. Many do a great job of presenting a warm environment with attentive and friendly staff. However, for a variety reasons they are not for everyone. Around two-thirds of people with a terminal condition choose to receive hospice care in their homes rather than at such facilities. John and his wife, Kaitlin, were among those who made that choice.

Because most of my visits are to facilities that are spotlessly clean and routinely scrubbed of the typical scents of peoples' lives, I wasn't accustomed to the mouth-watering aroma that greeted me as I entered John and Kaitlin's house. Something very good was cooking. Walking past the kitchen, the smell followed me into the living room where John was lounging, watching TV. After introductions, I asked Kaitlin about the delicious smell.

"Italian meatballs," she said. "I cook them every day for John."

Kaitlin, as a loved one often does, made the visit meaningful for all of us. When I asked each of them to tell me their favorite bands and singers, Kaitlin rattled off a number of names that included Johnny Cash, Ray Charles, Peter, Paul and Mary, and a few other late 1950's and early 1960's artists. John just smiled in agreement. I played random songs from some of these artists and Kaitlin knew the words to every one of them. Sitting next to John on their couch, she held his hand, looked into his eyes, and gently wept as she sang to him. I wondered if each song was a marker from the early stages of their relationship. I had never experienced that level of emotional intimacy or tenderness between a client and a loved one.

John moved his lips to some songs and sometimes tapped his feet. That's about all his condition would allow. After about five songs, I asked if they could remember where they were and what they were doing when these songs were popular. John, who couldn't speak very well, mumbled, "Oklahoma City." Kaitlin had been working and living at home with her parents.

I then asked how they had met. She said, "On a church hayride." She added that John's favorite song at that time was "Hit the Road Jack" by Ray Charles, a tune I had recently learned.

"How long have you been married?" I asked.

She said, "Fifty-seven years. We were married in 1963." She said that on the night of the hayride, she told her mother she had met the guy she was going to marry, and her mom told her she was crazy. I watched John squeeze her hand.

Before I left their home, I commented once again on the great smell of the meatballs. She said there was a batch in the oven, and that the freezer and refrigerator were stuffed with them.

Also, she and John couldn't eat them all or give them away fast enough. "Then, why are you cooking more?" I asked. She told me the smell of the meat and sauce made John relax. He loved that smell. She explained that as his condition progressed, his sense of smell and taste was diminishing. I don't know how it occurred to her, but she thought if she cooked and fed him regular doses of meatballs smothered in sauce, something of the aroma and taste would get through.

Before I left, Kaitlin insisted I take a big bag of meatballs with me.

Aromatherapy is administered by some hospices as a therapy for symptoms of dementia, including anxiety, trouble sleeping, and even memory and cognitive function. These volatile oils, which are distilled or cold-pressed from rosemary, lemon balm, lavender, peppermint, and other plants, are commonly used. These fragrances are believed to contribute to a patient's well-being. Diluted with carrier oils, they can also be applied to the skin and incorporated in touch therapies.

Apparently, the scent of lovingly prepared meatballs is equally therapeutic.

When I first became a bedside musician, it never occurred to me that playing music and interacting with dying folks might require entering the very private space of strangers at a time when they were most vulnerable, preparing to leave behind their known lives for an uncertain destination, even as they clung to their memories. I slowly learned to become vulnerable with them too. Participating in one of the most tender moments of others' lives through songs and companionship would often leave me also feeling this way. It was in this state, that I experienced the slow emergence of pieces of my own past, percolating up through lost times of my own life.

At fourteen, I began retreating further into my music. Almost all my friends were musicians. By fifteen, I had formed a band. We weren't great, but we were good enough to perform in public and earn a little money. I was the band's lead guitarist and business manager. It was my job to find us paid opportunities to perform. I figured this also made me the band's leader. Taking charge of our affairs, as if I were the boss, I compulsively planned our activities, from band practice days to the songs we should learn to play. My take-charge attitude culminated in a small revolt as the band approached a date I will never forget.

On November 2, 1968, Eric Clapton and Cream would play at Madison Square Garden. Everybody knew this would be one of their last U.S. performances before breaking up a month later and everyone's last opportunity to see them play together. Shortly after purchasing our tickets, I secured our band's first gig at a Rutgers University fraternity, something I had been working on for months. I knew that once we played at one fraternity weekend party, doors would open to others. Unfortunately, it was the same night as the Cream concert.

Explaining that this party could lead to future gigs to my band members, I suggested we sell our Cream tickets so we could play it. They unanimously said no. I was mad and uncompromising until I got my way. It turned out I was correct, that gig led to a busy schedule of appearances at other university fraternities and my band mates forgave me. I had convinced myself that I had earned their respect by not standing down. As for Eric Clapton, I finally got to see him perform forty years later.

I had learned that a combination of anger and sound reasoning got peoples' attention and that provided me confidence. I had plenty of it to channel into my activities. My mom's behavior was growing stranger and stranger all the time. Her fears and delusions were more frequent and intense. She'd spend hours a day just staring at the walls in our home with no conversation followed by irrational outbursts.

That was also about the period when an old delusion re-emerged. Her phone calls to the White House angrily demanding money became more frequent. In fits of frustration, I would pull our only phone out of its wall base and yank out all the wiring. Of course, without a phone, no car, and no adult friends or relatives checking on us, we were left more isolated than ever. No matter, she'd eventually call the phone company to reinstall the phone and her crazy calls would resume until the next time I yanked the phone out of the wall. I was about fifteen when these episodes occurred. With each one, my brothers seemed to disappear.

On occasion, a friend would drop by to see me, usually a member of my band. Years later I learned that my friends had all sensed something was wrong with my mother and my home life. They also noticed that I'd be punished by her for little infractions that she escalated into major crises of disobedience. My response was to increasingly disobey, or even provoke her out of revenge for the bizarre behaviors and overall craziness I had endured. I was only vaguely aware that she was suffering but it didn't matter. Today I am ashamed at how very satisfying it was to torment her. I've regretted this for years.

Because my brothers and I were all so young, I don't think any of us initially connected the dots. In other words, we knew nothing about mental illness. We were accustomed to rarely going anywhere, not having visitors to our home, taking no family vacations, and having no gatherings with aunts, uncles, and cousins, most of whom we would never again see or recognize. This was our normal life. However, these things have a way of catching up with you emotionally.

I didn't recognize it at the time, but I was experiencing very deep depression almost daily, lying awake most nights unable to sleep because there was an indefinable cloud in my head. I had no idea what my younger brothers were feeling because none of us talked much. And anyway, most little kids can't express these emotions in words.

With our father out of the house except for his once-a-week custody day, we had few adult examples of what it was like to have ongoing conversations that made any sense. The recipe for future emotional problems as adults was by now firmly in place. My teenage response to the chaos in my household was a deep immersion into drugs, music, and rebelliousness.

5 The Unlikely Hippie

If music is a place—then jazz is the city, folk is the wilderness, rock is the road, classical is a temple.

—Vera Nazarian

Name: Joan
Age: Unknown
Diagnosis: End-stage cardiac disease

The first time I played for a terminally ill patient, I had no idea what to expect. The volunteer manager at the hospice sent me to a nursing home to play for a woman diagnosed with end-stage cardiac disease. I was a bit nervous, not knowing what I might encounter. Would the patient be bedbound, in a wheelchair, conscious, unconscious, in pain? What if she disliked the music? Although I had been trained by my hospice to deal with a variety of situations, all that training became a blur.

Because many hospices are quite sensitive to the concerns and experiences of their volunteers, I was not expected to do this first visit by myself. My volunteer manager attended and also arranged for the patient's team manager to be present. The team manager is the leader of an individual patient's care team. Their function is to supervise, evaluate, and coordinate the various component members of the interdisciplinary team assigned to each patient. The team may consist of a nurse, medical director, social worker, and chaplain if the patient has spiritual needs. Volunteers like me work as needed. The team manager assures continuity of care for clients and families. I was aware that I'd be observed to see how the patient responded to my music and how well I would interact with her.

When I entered the room, Joan was sitting in a wheelchair with something of a scowl. As she looked me over, I tried to warmly introduce myself and share a little of my background. Making small talk, I sized up the situation and what songs to play. Less than five minutes into our chat, she abruptly cut me off, saying, "Okay, let's see what you got!" That's when I let her know that I don't sing, that I'm an instrumental guitarist who plays a lot of soft, soothing music. She cut me off again, basically wanting to know what was wrong with me. "You play for people but don't sing!?" (I have heard this more than a few times.)

I quickly realized that Joan was going to be a challenge. Seeing how feisty she was, I insisted she just relax and give the music a chance. My first song was the 1960 hit tune "Spanish Harlem" by Ben E. King. It's a nice, soft tune that I often start with because it's very familiar to most people of all ages. It wasn't long before she silently moved her lips to the melody, something I have also often seen with other clients.

Before I could finish the song, Joan gave me a surprise when she aggressively interrupted me to ask if I could play for the entire nursing home during their dinner. "It's hotdog and chili night!" she proclaimed. She insisted that I stay and play for everyone and let me know that "YOU'LL HAVE TO PLAY VERY LOUD. EVERYONE HERE IS DEAF!" Thus, I was escorted to the dining area where I waited with my guitar as patients entered the room.

I had a great time giving that concert and so did the patients. My last exchange with Joan went something like this.

Her: Play something from my generation.

Me: What would that be?

Her: Woodstock.

Me: No way . . . that's not your music!

Her: How would you know?

Me: Because no one there looked like you! Name me one song from that era.

Her: Nope! You figure it out.

We went on like this for a while, until I departed.

No two clients are alike, and each has a story, whether they can share it or not. Depending on their condition, people in hospice may be fully alert and full of humor. Some, like Joan, will tease you gently and playfully. Being open to the unexpected may invite surprises like Joan.

Joan was taken off hospice care a few months later, having made a recovery. Aside from experiencing my first hospice client, playing for the dining hall group helped me to overcome a long time fear I had about playing solo for groups of people and the potential of being rejected by any of them. Playing with a band, you get to hide behind others who may drown out your mistakes. I had stage fright.

By my junior year in high school, in addition to playing rock music with my regular band, I was also in my high school jazz band learning to play iconic songs like "In the Mood," "A Night in Tunisia," "Take the 'A' Train," and "Ain't Misbehavin'." I also hooked up with a local dance band. There were four of us— guitar, drums, trumpet, and accordion. Most of our repertoire was from the '30s, '40s, and '50s. I found much of the music to be corny and "for old people," songs like "Pennies from Heaven," "Sentimental Journey," "Fly Me to the Moon," "Sunny Side of the Street," "Over the Rainbow," and "Swinging on a Star." I was certain that no one we played for listened to Jimi Hendrix, Cream, the Rolling Stones, or the Who.

I think the reason I stayed with the group was that eventually the music grew on me. More than that, however, the money I earned was huge for a sixteen-year-old at that time. Most weekends we played at weddings, anniversaries, birthday parties, and in small dance halls for people my parents' age or older. These dates all paid more than the gigs with my rock band, about $75, versus $50, per musician. I was the band's anomaly, a longhaired, beads-and-bell-bottoms kind of guy. The others wore crew cuts and white short-sleeved, button-down dress shirts. They were strait-laced guys, just like the typical audience members.

At about the same time, I became a thespian. That was a cool-sounding name for kids who acted in school plays. I was issued an official Thespian Society ID card with my name and a serial number, making it appear that I was a member of an exclusive international organization for actors. A few of the school's greasers and other ignorant assholes called us fags. The greasers were typically White working-class kids who dressed in 1950's rockabilly fashion and wore a pompadour hairstyle using some type of petroleum-based product, just like in the movie *Grease*. Today this would be called retro. Back then, they were simply out of touch.

When not expanding my musical vocabulary, I was expanding my consciousness with every legal or illegal drug I could obtain—I could afford them now that I was making some money. Sniffing glue; smoking pot, hashish, and opium; and dropping diet pills, mescaline, peyote, and LSD. These are the ones I can recall. If I could swallow or smoke it, I was all-in.

My friends and I actually even tried smoking dried banana peels. We thought the lyrics to the Donovan song "Mellow Yellow" suggested this as a way to get high. That only resulted in a lot of coughing and sore throats.

Any notion I might have had that my parent's divorce would ease the tension in our family was put to rest as my mother's illness progressed. Now divorced for a couple of years, my father, who tried to steer clear of her, would become part of her delusions. She often described him as being crazy and referred to him as a "lazy beast that foamed at the mouth." She was constantly pressing him for an increase in child support. He would proudly threaten to go to jail rather than pay her more money, which did not do much for his sons' sense of security.

The reality that my mother was possessed by her hatred was on full display the night of my first performance in a school play. The play was the musical *You're a Good Man, Charlie Brown*, based on the popular Peanuts comic strip. I played the part of Linus, sort of the spiritualist in the cast of kids. He relies on the magic of his security blanket and faith in the eventual appearance of the Great Pumpkin. On opening night, my father showed up to watch, taking a seat in the last row of the auditorium. During the second act, as I was saying my lines, there was a commotion in the theater. I scanned the dark hall from the stage and spotted my mother. She was standing behind my father, beating him over the head with her purse. Upon entering, she must have seen him and gone into a rage.

Oddly, I have no memory of feeling embarrassed. I remained calm, taking the episode in stride without pausing my lines, and quickly got back into my character. No one ever mentioned it to me—neither schoolmates nor teachers. My father never said anything or apologized either. Of course, my mother moved on to her next emotional distraction. I quickly retreated to my safe haven of detachment and denial of my family being unusual in any way.

I was proud of my role in the play and especially of the standing ovation I received when taking my bow. I was eager to get back on stage in future plays so I could disappear into the characters I would play.

6 Messy Rooms

Where words fail, music speaks.

—HANS CHRISTIAN ANDERSEN

Name: Florence
Age: 87
Diagnosis: Kidney failure and dementia

A large number of my clients are nonresponsive to my presence. These seem to mostly fall into two types of patients. First are those whose condition has left them unable to display verbal or physical engagement at a discernable level during my time with them. The others appear to be sleeping throughout my visit, possibly too tired, weak, or medicated for anything else. Music and conversation may or may not be registering with both of these groups.

I think Florence was in the latter group: the sleepers. From the time I entered her room until I walked out the door, she appeared to be peacefully sleeping in her bed. Upon my arrival, I gently said hello to see if she was actually awake and just not responding. She didn't open her eyes or shift into another lying position. The first few times I encountered this with clients, I would play a couple of soft songs and talk to them. If there was still no visible engagement by then, I would pack up and leave. My mindset was such that I didn't want to waste my time if no one would be hearing the music I played. I figured I had better things to do with my time if there would be no applause or expressed satisfaction from my audience.

My attitude changed with Florence. As I sat in her room playing music, it registered that I wasn't volunteering my time for my own need to be recognized and appreciated with every musical appearance. I became hopeful that just my presence might be beneficial on some level to each client, even if not all were aware of my being there. Maybe the music was getting through and maybe not. It suddenly didn't matter.

During that visit, I became very aware of Florence and her surroundings. As I played the guitar, I reflected upon what her life might have been like and what kind of person she might be. Initially, I just stared at her, noticing something elegant in her facial features. They were very sharp. She must have been very beautiful when she was younger.

I then scanned the room, which was quite messy. She practically had a minimart in her room: three types of M&Ms, Kahlua-flavored chocolates, three bags of cheddar Goldfish and an open family-size bag of Cheetos. These and other snacking delicacies must have been her comfort food. They sat on the tops of dressers and on two bedside nightstands.

Around her small room someone had placed framed photos that were snapshots of another era. Most were of young adults with 1940's and 1950's hairstyles and clothes, at what appeared to be social events like weddings or graduation parties. The one that really got my attention was of an attractive teenager in a poodle skirt who looked a lot like Florence.

The room where Florence would likely die was suddenly warm and inviting. Instead of looking at my watch every few minutes to see how much more time I had to spend with her, I relaxed, and my mind eventually wandered into a certain time and space of my own teenage years.

The few children of a mentally ill parent who grow up to be healthy, high-functioning adults are usually those in the regular company of the healthy other parent or another caring relative. Children who interact daily with a healthy adult have fewer problems partly because they have a reference point for what is reality and what is misperception and which types of behavior are or are not appropriate. My brothers and I had no such regular interactions. Other than a regular midweek phone call, we only saw our dad occasionally, usually on custody weekends. When we did see him, we didn't do much talking—mostly TV watching. I haven't a single memory of my father discussing our family situation with us as kids (or even when we became adults).

Years later, in my late twenties and struggling with emotional issues, I asked him why he left us to be raised by our mom. I distinctly remember that phone call. His short response was, "Back then, men never took their kids in a divorce."

I then said I had begun seeing a psychologist to help me work through my problems.

He replied, "Kids today just aren't as sturdy as they used to be."

Such quick empty responses left me feeling wounded. What I really wanted was an apology or the admission of a colossal fuckup on his part. I am still mad that I could have said something like, "Most men would not have left their kids alone with a mentally ill person!" It might have made all the difference for some sense of closure for me, letting him contemplate his oldest son's rejection of him over his flimsy excuse for being a lazy negligent parent.

As an adult, my brother Mitch had several sharp conversations with Dad that ran along those same lines. These occurred after Mitch began facing his own emotional challenges. He put the blame on our father for his personal lifelong struggles, not on my mom who was simply sick.

My brothers and I still discuss this when we get together. What was our dad thinking? Or was he thinking at all? Today, his behavior might be considered child abandonment. In many states, it's a felony.

One of the mysteries about our father was how he came to be so persistently broke. He was college educated with a degree in accounting and a registered CPA with a well-paying job. But he never balanced his own checkbook and regularly bounced checks. Also, he never had any savings. It all seemed to be at odds with his professional skills. When we were children, he would often borrow (and never return) the small gifts of money that my brother Mitch would occasionally receive from visiting relatives as soon as they were out of sight. Stu recalls having a paper route in sixth grade. Each week he'd drop his five dollars in earnings into a jar. It ultimately became our dad's personal piggybank with no explanation on why he was taking it.

Eventually, when the money he took became larger sums, the borrowing felt more like stealing. When my mother became so sick that she could no longer take care of Stu, he went to live with Dad. Stu recalls how the $100 monthly social security disability checks he still received as a dependent of our disabled mother would simply disappear from the mailbox. These funds had been earmarked for his college education. Our father never mentioned his "borrowing" until quizzed.

The worst for me was the missing $1,700 in bar mitzvah gift money I received when I turned thirteen. Aware of Dad being accused of embezzling money by an employer only added to the intrigue about his money habits.

Oddly, none of us boys seemed mad at him for this weakness. I think we all viewed it (and maybe still do) as his blind spot and mostly shrugged it off because we knew he loved us.

After Dad and Mom were divorced, he chose to live in the Colonial Motel less than two miles from our home. At $7 dollars a night it was the type of lodging that transients called home when they could scrape together enough money for a few nights. It was also considered an inexpensive stop for tired overnight travelers. But it was definitely not a typical permanent home for a white-collar worker with children, like my father. I believe now that it was all he could afford.

Starting when I was about sixteen, I began walking there in the evenings every couple of weeks. It took about thirty minutes on foot.

Dad's little room was a bedroom and kitchen packed into to a cramped space the size of a small home office. I believe back then they called this unit an "efficiency." Whenever I arrived, he'd be in his underwear, relaxing on the double bed that filled most of the room. He'd almost always be smoking a cigar while watching a little black-and-white TV. In one corner was a small dinette furnished with a Formica-topped table and one chair. Across the room was a small sink and a kitchen counter just big enough to hold a double-burner hot plate. Below that, there was a mini refrigerator. The place was always a mess, with newspapers, magazines, empty fast food sacks, and half-eaten bags of potato chips and pretzels scattered about. It smelled strongly of pipe and cigar smoke. This was his afterwork lifestyle.

The room was way too cramped to accommodate all three of us brothers at once except for the briefest of visits, but it didn't matter because he made little effort to bring us there. Plus, there was the hurdle of him not having a driver's license. He had no easy way to come get us.

At the time, I was unfazed by the accommodations. I was thrilled every time I visited him by myself for occasional overnights. We didn't actually talk much beyond his asking about school and how that was going. I have no recollection of him sharing about himself. But that seemed okay and normal for us. Away from my crazy, depressed mom for at least one night every few weeks and always warmly welcomed, these were the few times I felt safe. I, escaping from my mother's disordered mind to my father's disorganized, disheveled room, was a giant step up. I even thought about asking Dad if I could move in with him. I fantasized that we would be two bachelors together making their way in the world, like on a TV sitcom. He lived there for most of my high school years.

I have one distinct musical memory of an evening with him. My father had a small clock radio next to my side of the double bed. That was where I first heard a band called The Moody Blues. The song was "Nights in White Satin." Through the years, whenever I hear a Moody Blues song, I think about me and my dad and the occasional cocoon of that motel room.

7 On Hearing

*Music produces a kind of pleasure that
human nature cannot do without.*

—CONFUCIUS

Name: Maude
Age: 88
Diagnosis: Stroke

Maude appeared to be sleeping when I arrived. I softly greeted her but received no verbal or physical acknowledgment of my presence. Her eyes were closed and there was almost no movement the entire time I played, just her chest barely moving up and down from her breathing, which seemed to be very shallow. This was a shared room arrangement and her roommate, however, was racing around the room in a wheelchair; worrying about how many songs she would miss because she had to leave to go play Bingo in the activities center. She was very chatty and loved the music. None of her noisy movement seemed to disturb Maude, whom I assumed was medicated.

When my bedside performance ended, I whispered goodbye, hoping not to disturb Maude. She immediately opened her eyes, slightly smiled, and whispered back, "Thanks." I reached out as if I were going to gently touch her hand and she lifted hers, meeting mine halfway. That was her only gesture during my visit.

It's one of the mysterious things about playing for those who may be extremely near the ends of their lives. They may seem unconscious, displaying no sign of engagement, but something may be getting through. I've experienced a similar scene many times.

Hearing is thought to be the last sense that goes in the dying process, depending on the type of death. I have heard that your eyesight may diminish near death and goes when you lose the strength to keep your eyelids open, and that your sense of touch may diminish as your blood pressure drops because blood is reserved for the brain and heart. Perhaps since your ears are close to your brain, they will have a decent blood supply as long as your brain has blood.

Also, it takes no physical strength to operate the ears.

Although healthcare professionals almost universally accept hearing as the last functioning sense, I've read that this has not been scientifically proven. It simply can't be conclusively verified by existing medical technology. While there is often measurable brain activity during the last moments of dying and even for a brief time afterward, that may be a reaction to a momentary release of brain-generated chemicals, not a response to hearing.

Or, as I have come to believe, it may be the manifestation of a spiritual transition beyond our comprehension.

None of these explanations precludes the possibility of music being perceived near the time of death.

HIGH SCHOOL WAS A BLUR since I was high on drugs during so much of class time. Other than music and rehearsing for plays, I had little to keep me productively busy. I hated sports. That was the main interest of a jock culture whose members mostly looked down upon those of us who were labeled as hippies. Many saw me and my friends as unpopular losers. For my part, I believed these kids were leftovers from the closeminded era of the 1950s. I based my judgment of them on the way they dressed and their outdated crewcut or pompadour style haircuts.

During the Vietnam War, their mantras were "America, love it or leave it" and "My country, right or wrong." These were common responses to a growing movement that was protesting the Vietnam War. Dissenters were considered unpatriotic or un-American. Some of these kids and their parents were also homophobic, anti-Semitic, racist bullies with distorted ideas about Black and Latinx folks.

Like most of my peers, I figured a new mentality fueled by a more tolerant outlook would soon wash these folks away. I was wrong about how entrenched their attitudes were.

The reality of that era was complicated. For every hippie, there was a hawk. The antiwar counterculture did not define the age. It simply had the largest media presence. The number one political song of the 1960s was not an antiwar anthem, of which there were many. It was "The Ballad of the Green Beret." Sung by a member of the Army Special Forces, it extolled red, white, and blue valor, strength, and patriotism.

During high school, my disgust with our country's leadership combined nicely with my growing animosity toward my mother.

It would turn out to be a potent concoction that created detachment and defiance of any authority figure: parents, teachers, religious leaders, business elites, and especially the government criminals who ended up sending 58,000 Americans to their deaths in Vietnam. I placed them all into the same category of human being that included my classmates who joked about gays, African Americans, hippies, and others of "difference." It became easy for me to resist, challenge, or reject all forms of authority. Of course, I had the practice of an expert with my mother coping mechanism fully ingrained. I knew never to assume that people who are in charge know what they are doing just because they are in charge.

Later on, the same mistrust would be transferred to my college professors, employers, and girlfriends. A guiding philosophy was that no one else's truth should be held in higher esteem than my own as all knowledge is merely subjective opinion. Better to just rely on my own instincts and perception of reality and take the opinions of others with a grain of salt, I figured.

Rebelliousness was more or less captured by many of my generation in the culture of the late 1960s. The difference was that my outlook was slightly more intense, twisted by the frustration and emotional damage from living with a lunatic at home. I had built a comfortable wall to keep folks out, not realizing that I would become its prisoner. I remained that way—self-imprisoned, emotionally barricaded—for much of my adult life.

It is said that the Woodstock Music and Art Fair was the preeminent cultural marker of the 1960s, which were my coming-of-age years. This gathering of over 400,000 people over a hot August weekend in 1969 is popularly viewed as a sign of the final emergence of a different kind generation. I was there. It wasn't.

I was sixteen that summer between my junior and senior years in high school. I recall asking my mother for a few dollars so that I'd have some pocket money for food while at the festival. Yelling at me for even asking, I said, "Fuck you," and left the house, slamming the glass door so hard that it shattered. That act of uninhibited disdain for her felt like freedom. It marked the end of any civility or sensitivity I would show her for years.

With two friends, I drove from central New Jersey to upstate New York. My butt sure hurt, sitting in the middle of the backseat of a 1967 Mustang. It took about five hours on the Garden State Parkway and New York Thruway to make what should have been a two-hour drive because of the highway congestion caused by tens of thousands of vehicles going to the same destination.

The Woodstock Festival was a glorious mess. But even with little food or drinking water and no shelter, I felt happy, although sweaty and stranded on a muddy field from consecutive days of heat and rain. This much-heralded punctuation mark of the 1960's youth culture would be no more than an excuse to get high and hear a lot of great bands within an atmosphere marketed as a weekend of peace and harmony. In reality, it was a big party with huge promoter profits on the back end coming from the post-festival film rights, books, music soundtrack sales, and various product-licensing agreements.

The one product that no one thought to create might have been Essence of Woodstock, an aroma blended from a mixture of patchouli, pot fumes, and perspiration.

Within five years, guys were cutting off their long hair, the Vietnam War would wind down, and folks were finishing college or beginning careers. With little to protest, a new age of material greed was brewing. Sixties political and cultural values would be ingrained yet creating a more traditional life was the eventual path. The idea of the Woodstock Generation would soon be more of a romanticized myth than an actual cultural marker.

As for me, I left the festival a day early. Back home, I once again told my mother to go fuck herself. I changed out of my dirty festival clothes and left immediately for the Asbury Park Convention Center, a small theater on the New Jersey coast that seated about 3,000 people. There I saw a new band I'd been hearing about: Led Zeppelin.

8 Whooppee! We're All Gonna Die

Well, come on all of you, big strong men
Uncle Sam needs your help again
He's got himself in a terrible jam
Way down yonder in Vietnam
So put down your books and pick up a gun
We're gonna have a whole lotta fun.

And it's one, two, three
What are we fighting for?
Don't ask me I don't give a damn
Next stop is Vietnam
And it's five, six, seven
Open up the pearly gates.
Well there ain't no time to wonder why
Whoopee! we're all gonna die.

—Joe McDonald, "I Feel Like I'm Fixin' to Die Rag," 1965

Name: Sally
Age: 71
Diagnosis: Ovarian cancer

Sally was one of the youngest clients I had seen. Just a few years older than me, being with her made me self-conscious about my own mortality. That happens sometimes when I am with clients who are close to my age. She had been in hospice care for about a month when we met, having received her diagnosis shortly before that; and she was told that she had just weeks or, at most, a few months to live.

Most clients are told that a bedside musician will be arriving a day or two in advance of the scheduled visit. Some decline, their minds too far gone for it to register—for others it may be the highlight of their week. This was the case with Sally. She had been eagerly waiting for me.

Upbeat and chatty from the start, I found her to be highly articulate and witty; she loved laughing at her own jokes. Sally was also very musically savvy. Although not a musician herself she possessed a wide range of musical tastes. She loved jazz, classic rock, folk, gospel, blues, and soul.

Sally was curious about me to a degree I had never experienced from a client. She wanted to know where I grew up, places I had lived, what kinds of jobs I'd had before I had retired to play music, my family background, and my religious beliefs. She even asked whom I'd voted for in the last presidential election. She was very proud of her career as a journalist covering local politics and the music and arts scene around Kansas City for a variety of community newspapers.

Both of us had been transplants to Kansas City many years earlier, having been born and raised elsewhere. She shared with me her favorite places in the city, which led us to a discussion of the city's historic Eighteenth and Vine jazz district. Along with New Orleans's Basin Street, Los Angeles's Central Avenue, and Beale Street in Memphis, the Eighteenth and Vine area had been a vibrant, Depression-era entertainment center that was the midwife to the birth of a new style of jazz that was infused with blues. Sally was a fan of all the artists that had made the district famous: Count Basie, Big Joe Turner, and Charlie Parker among them. She told me that Eighteenth and Vine had fallen to urban blight in the 1950s and 1960s and that most recent attempts to fully revive the area back into a jazz and entertainment destination had fallen flat due to local political corruption and financial malfeasance on the part of developers. She had a clearly stated mistrust toward local government.

Our corruption conversation somehow segued to her thoughts on President Donald Trump, whom she despised. She said, "He and his enablers are crooks turning the United States into a land of broken promises." Sally was a nonconformist, a social-justice advocate who exhibited a tone of defiance towards authority. On all subjects, she spoke with passion and conviction.

Between songs, we talked about our early lives. Born in 1948, she was raised in the small city of Fort Dodge, Iowa. Her burning ambition in her youth was to be a journalist, but her father said, "No, that's no profession for a woman." He forced her to give up a full scholarship at the University of Missouri, which is one of the premier journalism schools in the country. In 1967, her father sent her to a college in Ann Arbor, Michigan. He said that a woman needed to be able to support herself if she had no husband. Thus, he steered her into the school of nursing. It was the late 1960s.

Knowing Ann Arbor's reputation as a hotbed of anti-Vietnam War and antigovernment activity during those years, I decided to play and stream music from that time period, purposely choosing songs that had a social or political message: "Ball of Confusion" (The Temptations), "Fortunate Son" (Creedence Clearwater Revival), "Revolution" (The Beatles), "Back to the

Garden" (Joni Mitchell), and "The Times They Are A-Changin'" (Bob Dylan).

Sally lit up with each song. I asked her what her point of view was about the Vietnam War all those years ago. She told me stories of obtaining fake IDs for her draft-age friends and driving them across the Michigan border into Canada to avoid being called to serve in the military. She also shared how she almost got arrested at the 1968 Democratic National Convention in Chicago, where she went with friends to protest the war.

Finally, Sally pointed to the wall across from her bed and said nothing as she waited for me to respond. On it hung a poster-sized photograph that was probably about fifty years old. I recognized the person in the photo: It was Abbie Hoffman, a guy she had met in Ann Arbor who became a nationally known anti-Vietnam War activist and notorious antigovernment agitator. She idolized him. If only Sally's conservative father could see what she would become!

Before our musical visit ended, together we sang some verses to a somewhat obscure song from that era, one that momentarily captured our mutual rebellious spirit: Country Joe and the Fish's "I Feel Like I'm Fixin' to Die Rag."

I had four sessions with Sally over a six-week period. With most clients, I usually make just one or two visits. We bonded so quickly and deeply that she asked the hospice to bring me back as often as I was available. The feeling was mutual on my part. I knew time was running out and I wanted her to know how much I cared about her. To that end, I wrote her into this chapter of *The Music Between Us*. On our next visit, I told her I wanted to give her something special. Sitting at the end of her bed, I took out a copy of the manuscript pages and read them to her. We both cried. That had never happened to me with a client.

I left her with the pages, letting her know that when my book was released, I would give her a signed copy. Sally passed away three weeks after that visit. I think of her often and of all the music we listened to dating back to the late Sixties when revolution was in the air and I was separating from my family.

One of my greatest regrets looking back over events is that, as the eldest brother at home, my ongoing need to escape my inner turmoil kept me physically and emotionally separated from my younger brothers. By age fifteen, I was nowhere to be found. My basic daily routine consisted of going to school, returning home, and, within minutes, leaving again to be with my friends. Evenings were spent listening to music and doing drugs if any were available.

At about six o'clock every evening, my middle brother, Mitch, would call or come get me home for dinner. Typically, this would be an overcooked meal. Our mother by this time was incapable of paying attention to the details of planning and preparing meals. Also, she had become compulsively attached to certain routines and became upset with any variations to them. The result was that there was little variation to our meal plan, what we ate, and in what order. We had liver and onions on Monday, lamb chops on Tuesday, canned spaghetti on Wednesday, baked chicken on Thursday, fish sticks on Friday, and leather-tough steak and halibut on the weekend. Once in a while, we had canned peas. (Is there anything worse?) For years, we ate the very same seven meals, usually in that order.

Mom's decreasing ability to handle life's smallest details also extended to meal cleanup. She would never thoroughly rinse the soap off the dishes. Thus, we were drinking a fresh glass of soapy water at the next meal. Years later, while away at college, I was delighted with the quality of the school's cafeteria food while my freshman peers complained, longing for a good homecooked meal. Little did they know how good they had it.

When I was fifteen and beginning my drug-addled adventures with friends, my two brothers were just six and eleven years old. Stuck at home, they were too young to escape the weirdness of living with our mother. During their early years, it never occurred to me to try to stay close to them. First off, we were too far apart in ages to have much in common. It was too boring to hang out. Second, our mom was often alone in her bedroom sitting silently and staring off into space. There was literally no one at home with whom I could relate.

I still feel guilty about being the older brother who might have done something for them, or to just have been around, but it was not to be.

My escape occurred when I left for college. I could not have cared less about an education. I needed to get as far away as possible. It was a long way from an urban part of New Jersey to Milton, Wisconsin. Milton College was a tiny school of about 900 students in a small town with under 4,000 residents. I was initially surprised that, like me, about half of the student body were transplants from the Northeast. With a large contingent of hippies, political radicals, and dope smokers, I felt right at home.

Also, during my freshman year, I met Leslie, my first girlfriend. That made everything better and I rarely, if ever, gave my New Jersey family a thought. I was carefree for the first time in my life and beginning to move away from depression and the drugs that had kept me so occupied in high school. Being a good student and someone's boyfriend was a new life.

The first time I went home from college was during Thanksgiving of my freshman year. Within minutes of returning, I broke down and cried. Seeing my brothers, who were truly excited that their older brother had come home, along with my mom's eager anticipation of my presence, was just too emotional. I felt pressured. Their excitement didn't last long as I immediately fell into my old anxiety and habits upon arriving. After being gone for three months, it took me all of about sixty minutes to leave the house, declining the dinner Mom had prepared for that evening. I walked to a McDonald's just blocks from our home, where I ate in the comfort of solitude. I then arranged to spend most of my visit getting high with old buddies.

Returning home then quickly leaving resulted in both brothers' disappointment. But I had flipped into a state of such detachment when I returned to that house of pain that I was not aware of them having any of their own emotional issues. However, I figured that all the freedom and happiness I had gained by being almost 1,000 miles from home would return after I was back on campus. Yet, that was a mirage. Eventually, a sense of detachment from all others would emerge along with a variety of defense mechanisms to avoid genuine closeness with people. These behaviors would follow me for many years, in every relationship, personal and professional. It was baggage I had no idea I had been carrying.

Only in my forties did I make a genuine effort to reconnect with my two brothers. We had each gone our own way, settling in different parts of the country, rarely seeing one another. I learned that they too had had struggles as a result of our mutual upbringing.

After that Thanksgiving break, I would return to New Jersey just one more time. This was when I found out what life had become for them under our mother's care.

9 Eloise and Her Roommate

Any musical innovation is full of danger to the whole State, and
ought to be prohibited . . . when modes of music change, the
fundamental laws of the State always change with them.

—PLATO

Name: Eloise
Age: 100
Diagnosis: Unknown

About a quarter of the folks I visit as a bedside musician are in
semiprivate rooms at the facilities where they live. These are
shared living arrangements. This makes the cost of care more
affordable than having a private room. However, with another
patient in the room, someone typically with a different
diagnosis, things can get interesting, especially if the roommate
wants to engage with me in ways that annoy the client I am
scheduled to see.

Eloise was one of the oldest clients I had visited. I played for
her twice. She was bright eyed and listened intently to the music.
I observed her watching my left-hand move around the guitar
neck. After some songs, she'd hold up her left hand and splay her

very long fingers. At the same time, she moved her entire hand up and down an imaginary guitar neck and pretended, with her right hand, to pluck strings. She was imitating me.

I guess it was a version of playing air guitar alongside your favorite rock musician.

I asked what she was doing, and she said she was trying to figure out how I could hit so many strings so quickly without playing the wrong notes.

She was amazed.

I was amused.

At one point during our first visit, Eloise's roommate rolled her wheelchair around the room divider that separated them. She tried to engage me in light conversation. Thus, I actually had an audience of two people both times I played for Eloise.

During my second visit, the roommate continuously interrupted me in the middle of songs with questions. She was trying to get my name which she had forgotten from my first visit a few weeks earlier.

Roommate: "Please stop playing. . . . What's your name?"

Me: "Steve."

Roommate: "Mike?"

Me: "Steve."

Roommate: "Jim?"

Me: "No, STEVE!" (I raised my voice since she was clearly hard of hearing.)

Roommate: "Dennis?"

Me: "Sure."

After that exchange, she informed me that the real reason she wished to speak to me was to let me know she owned a forty-year-old bass ukulele that needed some repairs, and could I fix it for her? Eloise just rolled her eyes, as she patiently waited for me to play more music.

Near the end of the second visit, Eloise removed a photograph from her bedside drawer. It was a grandson killed in Iraq. She calmly said that she never understood why we were at war over there.

While she spoke, I noticed, for the first time, the largest rosary I have ever seen hanging on the wall next to her bed. It was probably around six feet long with prayer beads the size of small marbles on it. Attached to the top of the wall and hung by a nail, the bottom of the rosary reached the top of her bed with its crucifix dangling near her pillow.

I asked her about it, and she said, "It's been faith that's kept me alive so long."

I do not know much worship music, so for our last song, I streamed, "On Eagle's Wings" by Josh Groban. Before I left, Eloise asked me back for a third time, but she passed away before I could return.

For me, as with so many others, the music and culture of the 1960s were bookended by the Beatles. Their decision to break up near the end of 1969, followed by the release of their last record in early 1970, would close the window they opened in 1962. Their groundbreaking music indirectly fueled tradition-shattering shifts in popular culture, the pursuit of spiritual consciousness, and even political thinking. After they were gone, the great music they inspired kept expanding, both through the music of other 1960's bands and that of newer artists in the 1970s.

As I began college at the beginning of the new decade, music simultaneously went in opposite directions with the emergence of early heavy metal bands like Black Sabbath, Deep Purple, and Uriah Heep. This was in contrast to softer, more melodic songs produced by artists who are still icons of music, such as:

- "Take Me Home, Country Roads," John Denver

- "Fire and Rain," James Taylor
- "Bridge Over Troubled Water," Simon and Garfunkel
- "Tea for the Tillerman," Cat Stevens
- "Time in a Bottle," Jim Croce
- "Maggie May," Rod Stewart
- "It's Too Late," Carole King
- "Just My Imagination (Running Away with Me)," The Temptations
- "I'll Be There," The Jackson 5
- "American Pie," Don McLean

Anti-Vietnam protest music was also changing. In the 1960s, this music was plentiful but primarily not mainstream with some notable exceptions, like Barry McGuire's song "Eve of Destruction." This became one of the most popular songs the year it was released (1965) in spite of many radio stations refusing to play it for fear of alienating conservative listeners. This and Creedence Clearwater Revival's "Fortunate Son" (1969) both made it onto *Billboard* magazine's Top 100 list in their respective years.

Beginning in the 1970s, when Americans became exhausted by the number of body bags returning home from Vietnam, the volume on this type of music got dialed way up. Powerful new antiwar songs by both new and already famous artists found their way onto mass appeal radio stations and were performed on TV. Who can forget these Billboard list toppers?

- "War," Edwin Star, #1, 1970
- "What's Going On," Marvin Gaye, #2, 1971
- "Imagine," John Lennon, #3, 1971

In my first year of college, I buckled down to studying in tranquil Milton, and almost entirely stopped doing drugs.

However, this was not the lifestyle I found among many kids at school. Radical and rebellious, many of my new friends were playing with more serious drugs than I had ever tried in high school, drugs like heroin and methadone. One of the reasons I had left New Jersey was to get away from that behavior.

Aspects of my character that I am proudest of would be shaped during my freshman year. I was aware of conspiracies being hatched that were often violent ways to protest U.S. involvement in Vietnam. These conspiracies ran the gamut from defacing public property to blowing up campus buildings in order to make a defiant statement. My own interest in opposing the war was much more nuanced and peaceful in nature.

Soon after arriving at school, I met a Vietnam veteran who was beginning his junior year. He introduced me to the local chapter of a small, peaceful organization called Vietnam Veterans Against the War. I was accepted as a nonveteran supporter. With fewer than 1,500 members, VVAW exploded into a national organization when it aggressively publicized the mounting evidence of ongoing U.S. atrocities against civilians in Vietnam and the war's expansion into Cambodia. Part of its credibility lay in the fact that unlike most of the veterans of prior American wars, the VVAW vets were highly critical of U.S. policy in Southeast Asia. These vets were openly describing the atrocities they'd seen as a way to sway public opinion.

By 1971, VVAW's membership and active supporters like myself swelled into the tens of thousands as its activities quickly became very visible. I managed to join their rallies and marches in Milwaukee and Madison, handing out antiwar flyers.

Right-wing conservatives, at the time calling themselves the *silent majority*, labeled us as traitors. By publicizing and agitating against the war's atrocities, we considered ourselves patriots. President Nixon and the FBI did not. Thus, when I was informed that my name might be on an FBI enemies list, I got scared and withdrew my presence from all rallies and meetings. My name being on that list may have only been speculation, but I became a scared eighteen-year-old who quickly ceased openly protesting.

A year later, I would be called upon to take the military induction physical. This was not voluntary. With no doctor's note to verify that I had some trumped-up disqualifying condition like bone spurs, I sadly passed the physical. I thought a lot about moving to Montréal, Canada, where I had already made arrangements for lodging in case my number was called in the lottery, a system in which every draft eligible male was randomly assigned a number. The lower the number, the higher one's probability of getting drafted into military service.

My number was nineteen. Incredibly, I was spared going to war with a student deferment based upon my enrollment in college. I got lucky, as student deferments were limited in 1971. Over the following couple of years, the military draft was eliminated until the country adopted an all-volunteer military system.

By happenstance, VVAW celebrated its fiftieth anniversary in the same month I became a bedside musician. On its anniversary date, I played guitar in a nursing home for one hundred-year-old Eloise Hogan. That evening, I quietly toasted all Vietnam veterans, those who gave their lives and limbs, those who returned emotionally crippled or were criticized for serving in an unpopular war, and those who came home with the courage of their conviction to change minds and save lives.

10 Free Voice Lessons

Farther along we'll know all about it,
Farther along we'll understand why.
Cheer up, my brother, live in the sunshine,
We'll understand it all by and by.

"Faithful till death" saith our loving Master,
Short is our time to labor and wait.
Then will our toiling seem to be nothing,
When we shall pass the heavenly gate.

—ATTRIBUTED TO W.B. STEVENS, "FARTHER ALONG,"
ALTERNATE BARNEY E. WARREN, 1911

Name: Hollister
Age: 84
Diagnosis: Heart disease

The first thing I do when I arrive at a patient's room is give a little background about myself and find out what I can about them. Not all of them can speak, so this interaction can be a very brief or even one-sided conversation. I also check to see that I won't be disturbing a roommate. In this particular case, Hollister had one who was soundly sleeping with the covers over his head. I don't think he moved the entire time I was there.

I usually ask what kind of music the person I am visiting likes and also let the client know that I'm not much of a singer, so most of my music will be instrumental. We had started out quite nicely with our conversation until I told him this. Hollister leaned forward in his wheelchair and wanted to know, "What kind of guitar player doesn't sing?"

I quickly replied, "The kind that has a lousy voice!"

He then said, "Okay, play me some gospel music," at which point, I had to let him know that I only knew a couple of gospel songs. Clearly annoyed, he wasn't pleased about getting a bedside performance by someone who not only couldn't sing, but also didn't know much of his favorite music. He was not happy.

Just when I was becoming persuaded that this visit might be a waste of his time, Hollister told me that he would sing all the songs and I should just try to follow along on the guitar. I agreed to do so, figuring this might be quite entertaining for both of us.

Hollister had an incredible voice, deep and gravelly and very soulful. For about the next thirty minutes, we played some of the standard hits of old-time gospel and traditional hymns, me stumbling along on songs like "Just a Closer Walk with Thee," "Amazing Grace," and "Farther Along." I asked him if he had sung at his church. That's when he informed me that he used to tour with a southern gospel recording group.

Like most clients I meet (and the rest of us), he had a story to tell and his was about his touring days. He also named some albums he had recorded years earlier.

Before I left, Hollister encouraged me to practice my singing and then come back and see him for some tips on "improving your shitty voice."

Growing up, I was not even aware of gospel music and had no familiarity with traditional Christian hymns. Not just because I was Jewish, but because it was not the kind of music one heard on mainstream commercial radio stations in the New York City region. I suppose if one wanted to hear that kind of music one had to find a Baptist or Black Methodist Episcopal Church. These probably represented just a fraction of the region's churches.

The end of freshman year in Wisconsin found me in New York City. My Uncle Fred, my father's sister's husband, got me a summer job at his company and offered to house me. I lived with him on an upper floor of a high-rise apartment in Forest Hills, Queens. By the end of that summer, we were barely on speaking terms. Fred had all kinds of suggestions and advice about how I should spend my time, find girls, and take care of his apartment whenever he went away. He also expressed a lot of unfavorable opinions about my dad, telling me regularly about how irresponsible and undependable he was, and that he couldn't be trusted with money. Also, that he was lazy. No one had ever said these kinds of things to me about my father before, and I was offended.

Looking back on it now, I knew at the time that Fred was right, but I just couldn't admit it to myself or to my uncle. Nevertheless, I resented him for his bold, albeit truthful opinions and the embarrassment they caused me. He could have been much kinder to me. But he wasn't. Triggered, I snapped at him, and he began to see me as an irresponsible kid, someone just like my dad.

That summer, I mainly steered clear of Uncle Fred. He would leave every weekend to join my aunt during their three-month-long summer vacation in New York's Catskill Mountains. Thus, we didn't see one another all that often. Grateful that I didn't have to go home to New Jersey for summer break, I had lots of time alone to do nothing at all or to explore the city and reflect on what seemed like a new life of unfolding independence.

In July 1971, America's leading jazz ambassador, Louis "Satchmo" Armstrong died. In spite of his wealth and fame, he had chosen to live in the working-class neighborhood of Corona, Queens, less than three miles from my uncle's apartment in Forest Hills. American jazz became an art form due in part to his trumpeting and vocals. No one really knows where his nickname came from, but I have read that because of his large mouth, he might have been nicknamed "satchel mouth," which got shortened to Satchmo.

Being raised in a different musical era, I hadn't realized how many of the songs he was famous for singing in his raspy voice had become iconic American tunes until all the tributes that summer. Armstrong sang songs like "Ain't Misbehaving," "Georgia on My Mind," "On the Sunny Side of the Street," "Star Dust," "You'll Never Walk Alone," "When You're Smiling," "When the Saints Go Marching In," "Hello, Dolly," and "What a Wonderful World." These were composed by American greats likes Fats Waller, Hoagy Carmichael, and Jerry Herman. If you were someone who had not known much about Armstrong until then, your ignorance would have ended with the news coverage, TV specials, and memorials. Only the great artists with a sense of humor can get away with a statement like this: "There is two kinds of music, the good, and the bad. I play the good kind" (Louis "Satchmo" Armstrong).

Although I deliberately tried to stay away from my home in New Jersey that summer, it did get back to me that my mothers' condition had worsened. Previously, while I was still in high school, she had been committed to a state mental hospital, and I suppose the therapy and medication did her some good. When she returned home, she was almost unrecognizable—in a good way. She was less disoriented, more lucid, less delusional. However, the changes didn't last. Within a month she had stopped taking her meds and drifted back to her prehospitalization condition.

While on summer break, I heard that Mom had been chasing my brothers around the house with a knife in her hand, so I figured I had to take some action. I decided to have her committed again. The laws in New Jersey were crystal clear: You couldn't simply commit someone to a mental health facility based on your own judgment. (Certainly, that would be a nifty way to punish or dispose of folks we don't like.) It required the consensus of two doctors to commit someone, and they would handle the details with the hospital. I managed to get that done through family doctors who knew my mother. Because my father had agreed to stay with my brothers while she was hospitalized, I had few concerns about their safety.

Once the arrangements were made, all that was needed was to get her away from my brothers long enough to have her captured. This would not be a voluntary thing on her part. Today what we did would be called an *intervention.*

It went down like this: I phoned Mom and said I wanted to come visit and take her to a park for a walk so we could spend some time together. She was delighted. I picked her up at our New Jersey home, drove to the park, and we walked to a predesignated spot where a white unmarked van was waiting near a parking area. As we turned the corner of a walking trail, four uniformed guys quickly pulled up, jumped out of the van, grabbed her, placed her into a straitjacket, and strapped her to a gurney. She was shocked by all this and immediately freaked out. The last thing that I remember was her being scared and angry.

She asked, "Did *you* do this to me?"

I was shaken and shocked by this episode. At age eighteen, I had engineered an ambush of my own mother. She was admitted to the hospital for about two weeks before being set free, back on meds and much calmer. I immediately went back to the city to finish out the summer.

I didn't speak to my uncle for over twenty years. Eventually he mellowed and so did I. With my future wife's encouragement and a newly discovered spiritual viewpoint, I could finally accept that my uncle was actually trying to help me all those years ago.

11 The Graduate and the First Grader

Music, because of its specific and far-reaching metaphorical powers, can name the unnamable and communicate the unknowable.

—LEONARD BERNSTEIN

Name: Rosalyn
Age: 82
Diagnosis: Stomach cancer

Among the clients who are able to communicate, only a few express feelings about the transition they will soon be making. It is not a conversation I initiate because most hospices have experienced chaplains tending to the spiritual needs of patients and their families. The expression of religious beliefs or thoughts about the meaning of life and death are best left to the pros.

Rosalyn was one of my first clients as a new hospice volunteer. She would be the rare one who initiated such a conversation. My response was unsteady. I wanted to demonstrate my eagerness to listen, but only to share my own thoughts if asked directly. She wanted me to know that she was hoping that she had fulfilled whatever purposes God had for her and that she might "graduate with honors." It didn't matter to her if death was literally the end of everything or if there was a next leg of her journey.

Soon after my visit with Rosalyn, I attended what amounted to a "meet and greet" at one of the hospices where I volunteer. It was a way for the staff and managers to meet the volunteers, and for volunteers to get to know one another. At that meeting, I asked the hospice director, who also happened to be a chaplain, if recruiting volunteers to visit with dying patients was difficult. He said the greatest obstacle to recruitment was fear. He explained that volunteers might fear not knowing what to do if a patient is struggling, thinking they are supposed to assist them. Also, a fear of being present at the time a patient passes away often lurks under the surface.

The hospice director shared that, personally, he feels honored and privileged if he happens to be present at the time of someone's passing. He called it a *sacred moment.*

My impression, as he was describing his profound feelings about the death transition, was that it sounded almost like the joyful anticipation we might experience at the birth of a baby. But I sensed this was not typical. For most of us, one transition is associated with a life's beginning, the other with its ending. But is that really what's taking place—a joyful arrival and a joyful departure? Or is the beginning and end of each life just two transitions within a larger sequence of milestones in an eternal journey?

A few days after meeting the chaplain, I read an article in the *Washington Post* about a riddle given by a first-grade teacher to his class of six-year-olds.[1]

Puzzle of the Week

I am the beginning of everything, the end of everywhere.
I'm the beginning of eternity, the end of time and space.
What am I?

The answer the teacher was looking for was the letter E. However, one child's answer was "death."

Other guesses by students, included, "NOT everything," "All stuff," "The end," and his favorite, "Nothingthing."

Intentional or not, some of these first-grade answers had an existential element clearly absent from the correct answer. This classroom exercise really highlighted for me how we might see things on a deeper level than we often do, especially when it comes to questions about life and death. Is the primary discomfort we may possess at the idea of being present during the death of another actually an avoidance of contemplating our own passing?

Although we all know rationally of its inevitability, uncertainties about life and its aftermath, regardless of our religious beliefs, probably keep many of us from reflecting on a subject that may leave us with unease.

Some first-graders may know something we adults don't.

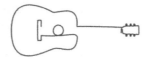

I HAVE BEEN A SPIRITUAL SEEKER all my life—though I did not understand this for a long time. I simply did not recognize the signs in my own actions and behaviors. Today, I practice seeking them in people, events, and daily situations in which I find myself. And still probably miss most.

Before I finished my first year of college at Milton College, I had made the decision to start my sophomore year at another school. The town and school were both too small for my taste and the tuition too high. My only requirement for the next move in my academic career was that it be a state school with low out-of-state tuition. I wanted to be as far away as possible from my mother's home in New Jersey—even further than Wisconsin. I also hoped for fewer East Coasters to remind me of home.

I did a search for any school in the country that fit these criteria and landed at Kansas State Teachers College in Emporia, Kansas. It was a school of about 6,000 in a town of 16,000. Out of thousands of schools in a directory of American colleges, this was by far the least expensive.

Emporia gave me culture shock; I hadn't expected its remoteness. Compared to my previous campus, there were hippies and left-wing political activists, but fewer of them. There were mostly in-state students, less aggressive personalities than the harder-edged ones I had met in Wisconsin—many of whom had been from back east, like me, and were culturally indistinguishable from the kids I grew up with.

At first, I hated Emporia, thinking I had made a mistake. It was too remote, stuck halfway between Wichita and Kansas City, and surrounded by seventy-five miles of wheat and cattle in the Kansas Flint Hills, with few towns in-between. There were too many farm kids and small-town folks. It was there that I met actual cowboys, kids who were from ranching families. Many people I met had never met a Jewish person and had little previous exposure to Blacks or other minority ethnic groups. So, I was somewhat of an oddity. Plus, I missed my girlfriend.

Miserable for about six months, I finally settled in with a few likeminded friends who mostly shared my taste in music and politics. I was also upbeat when my Wisconsin girlfriend, Leslie, decided to transfer schools and join me. We had gotten engaged shortly before I arrived in Kansas, so this seemed like the natural course of events.

I was just eighteen when I proposed to Leslie, with no idea what that really meant. She loved me and had told me she would follow me wherever I landed. Neither of us knew the risks of entering into a relationship with someone who had my family background.

Three years later, while she was making the wedding arrangements, I called things off. This would be the first of a number of long-term relationships that would go south.

One of the very surprising aspects of my time in Emporia was the faint hint of a spiritual awakening. Actually, it was more of a passing shadow—one so subtle that I didn't recognize it. Although raised in a Jewish family, I had no attachment to the faith of my birth. No one in my family ever said a prayer, attended synagogue, or even talked about God.

Mine was a purely secular existence. I was a deli Jew—big on the ethnic food, small on the theology. God had no place in my life. Years later, I determined for myself that if we don't find Him, God finds us. He leaves subtle signals or markers for us as we make our way through life. When our spiritual antennae are up, we may recognize these.

In my case, I had no antennae, and my receiver was probably not working very well. Thus, God must have taken a look in my direction and chose to turn up the volume slightly. Looking back, His first faint signal to me came soon after I arrived in Emporia, although I didn't clearly recognize it as such at the time.

Because I didn't own a car, I walked everywhere—often aimlessly wandering around Emporia's small downtown when I had nothing to do. It was late one summer evening when, during one of these strolls, I spotted a beautiful old stone Lutheran church. There was nothing particularly unique about it; it was just one of many in town. But I was drawn to it. Maybe it was the understated night lights planted around the building that gave it a warm glow.

I stopped to admire the architecture, walked up to the front door, and jiggled its handle. Finding it unlocked, I pushed the door open, entered, looked around the lobby, and then peered into the sanctuary. There was no one else there as I slowly walked into the quiet space, took a seat in that dimly lit room, and contemplated the peacefulness of the cross hanging high above the altar. It was softly lit from behind, creating a slight glow.

I was only there for about thirty minutes, but the experience of the church left me feeling an indescribable lightness for the remainder of the evening. When I left, I resumed my walk. I was nineteen years old and not fully aware of what I had encountered.

12 Ten-Minute Judy

If you were music,
I would listen to you ceaselessly
And my low spirits would brighten up.

—Anna Akhmatova, "March Elegies"

Name: Judy
Age: 95
Diagnosis: Short-term memory loss

Memory loss is one of the distinguishing signs of Alzheimer's disease. Short-term memory loss is one of its first symptoms. You might recall a loved one asking the same question multiple times in the course of a day. This is commonly described as the inability to recall information that was just recently given to you. The amount of time considered short-term varies; it can be anything from seconds up to a few days.

Although this is a serious condition for a patient, it can lead to some pretty amusing exchanges for a musician during a bedside performance. My first experience of this sort was with a delightful gal. When I informed her that I was mostly an instrumental player and only knew one song that I sing, she insisted that I play it. Afterward, we discussed the song at length. A few minutes later, she had already forgotten all about my one vocal song and wanted to know if I knew any songs that I could sing to her. So, again I played and sang that same song. She thought it was the nicest song she had ever heard and asked me about the words.

We repeated this identical exchange three times during my visit. It was a good way for me to practice my vocal abilities without boring my audience with the same song over and over.

Then there was Judy, another patient. Although she was told twenty-four hours in advance that I would be visiting, when I showed up the next day, she was delightfully surprised. She had no idea that a musician would be coming to see her! It turned out that Judy had almost no capacity for short-term memory.

I was a bit nervous about playing for Judy because I had been informed that she was a classically trained pianist. She even had a nice electric piano set up in her room. My concern was that being an amateur guitar player my simple songs might be boring to an accomplished musician such as herself.

The experience was lovely, however. Judy was very inquisitive; due to her memory lapses she kept repeating the same questions about every ten minutes: "Did you take lessons? How long have you been playing? Do you teach music? Did you ever play in a band?"

Judy was also intensely focused on my tee-shirt, which read WALNUT VALLEY FESTIVAL. A friend had picked it up for me at an annual finger-picking guitar competition that takes place in Winfield, Kansas. She must have thought it was an annual family reunion because she told me she thought she knew some folks named Walnut.

Judy turned out to be the perfect audience for me. She was very appreciative of the music and complimented me on my playing a number of times as she watched my fingers move up and down the guitar neck. When I asked her if she'd like to play me a song on her electric piano, she said, "No, I won't go near that piece of junk! I miss my baby grand piano."

We probably spoke as much as I played, and I felt at ease in Judy's company. I suppose, by itself, that was very comforting. I tried to get her to tell me about her own professional playing, but she didn't have much to say except when she leaned over and whispered, "Want to know a secret? People always thought I was much better than I really was!" She said this with a sly smile then giggled—a shared secret from one musician to another.

After quizzing me once again on our possible mutual connection to the Walnut family, Judy invited me to come back to talk and play for her. I replied, "Of course," knowing that with her memory issues, each future visit would essentially be the first—a new and exciting event for me as well. That's exactly what happened when I returned a couple of weeks later.

The link between song lyrics and long-term memory is still being deciphered but it's clear that familiar music can provide a memory jolt. Some dementia clients may suddenly come to life and sing the lyrics to songs without any prompting. Other cognitive functions also may be revived. Among the many conditions I encounter, dementia is the one which has captured my attention to the greatest degree. For me, there is something very foreboding about slowly losing one's memories or the recognition of familiar things, especially of friends and loved ones. It's as if our lives have slipped away when we are absent the experiences that have defined us.

The irony for me is that as I experience my own interactions with clients, my own long-buried memories sometimes come bubbling to the surface.

After completing college in Emporia, I headed to the University of Kansas in Lawrence to get a master's degree in East Asian Studies. It was 1975. After years of hostility with one another, the door between China and the United States had begun to open. The two nations began to trade with each other, and all sorts of potential business and exchange opportunities were waiting for Americans. I thought I might get a head start with a degree in East Asian Studies. The University of Kansas was the only school with a graduate studies program in this field to accept me.

Lawrence was just eighty miles up the road from Emporia, but culturally a world away. With about 25,000 American and international students, it was (for me) like landing in San Francisco after four years in a small farm town. The city had a vibrant music, art, and restaurant scene. It had been a hotbed of radicalism in the 1960s and early 1970s along with other college towns of that era, like Berkley, Madison, and Ann Arbor.

Although remnants of the 1960's counterculture were still present when I arrived, it was being displaced. Incoming freshmen and sophomores were more conservative in every way. No shoulder-length long hair on the guys and no tie-died ankle-length skirts on the girls. There was also no outrage about Vietnam to unify young people because the war was ending. In terms of music, fashion, and culture, the disco era had arrived.

I met Maria shortly after enrolling. It was at a *Star Trek* party. Based on the original TV series that had become a cult classic long before *The Next Generation* and other iterations, it was hosted by some student residents in my apartment building. Maria's apartment was almost directly across from my front door, but we never said more than "Hi" as we crossed paths. She came to the party as Lieutenant Uhura, I as Spock. We were two space travelers in awful homemade costumes and spent the entire evening talking and laughing.

Maria became the reason I broke off my engagement to Leslie. She was a gentle soul, studying to be an occupational therapist. With a Puerto Rican background, she had a Latin look that attracted me. The spark of a fresh love was struck. We ended up living together in Lawrence after I dropped out of grad school while she worked on finishing her own degree. My efforts to secure a master's degree in East Asian Studies were impeded by my inability to learn Mandarin Chinese. Now I see my goal was unrealistic.

After she graduated, we moved to Kansas City, the nearest major metropolitan area, where we shared an apartment and I settled into a retail job selling custom audio systems.

Fast forward. Maria and I had been together a couple of years and established a comfortable routine when my urge for something different emerged. Then, the fantasy of creating a new life somewhere else set in. When my company offered a promotion at a new store opening in San Antonio, Texas, I jumped at the chance, and I didn't ask Maria to come with me. In retrospect, I was oblivious about how such a decision would affect our relationship. I definitely didn't consider its immediate financial and emotional effects on her.

Maria quickly moved out of our apartment and into her own place. There was no discussion of issues such as what would become of us, whether she would one day join me, or if I planned to ever return to Kansas City. She probably knew I was not capable of an intimate conversation.

San Antonio was a disaster. First off, Maria had entirely given up on me after I'd been gone for a few months. She'd call me from Kansas City in the evenings, rarely finding me at home at any hour. Also, I never invited her to visit. I had quickly found a local girl to hang out with and did not come clean with either woman. Maria figured out what was up and sent me a Dear John letter. I was devastated when reading that she herself was having fun dating and no longer wished to be committed to a ghost. I knew that I deserved this outcome, but I still felt sorry for myself.

Yet, that wasn't the worst part of the San Antonio experience.

About three months after arriving, I got a phone call from my mother. She informed me that she was coming to Texas to live with me. She had sold the family home in New Jersey a year earlier and taken my youngest brother, Stu, to Miami, even though she had no relationships there. Stu was fifteen at the time.

My middle brother, Mitch, was already in his third year of college in Lawrence, Kansas. He had followed in my footsteps.

When Mom took Stu to Miami, I phoned my father and threatened never to speak to him again if he didn't rescue Stu. How, I asked, could he have left his youngest son in the care of a mentally ill person? He had no valid answer, but nevertheless brought him to Pennsylvania.

Completely alone then, and tortured by her worsening symptoms, my mother only lasted a few months longer in Miami when she recognized she could no longer take care of herself on her own. The money from the sale of the New Jersey house was gone and she was subsisting at poverty level on meager social security disability benefits.

During a brief phone conversation, Mom informed me that she would arrive in San Antonio in a week to move in with me.

With her condition worsening, I couldn't bear the thought of her coming to stay with me. Neither could my roommate, a guy who helped me pay the rent. I quickly warned him that my mother might be arriving to live with us and that I didn't yet have a plan. She might be with us for a while. When he asked me what she was like, I told him she was mentally ill. He threatened to move out if she was going to stick around.

I knew Mom's call was a plea for help. She had stopped seeing a psychiatrist and I figured she wasn't taking her medications either. She was frightened. But I immediately freaked out, feeling I was about to be thrust into a responsibility I couldn't handle. I tried to find a way to dissuade her from leaving Miami. The more I denied her self-invitation, the more hysterical she became. I was terribly abusive to her on that call. I simply had no compassion and wanted her to disappear as I always had.

Honestly, I don't recall who was more frightened: she, out of money and with nowhere to go or ability to take care of herself; or me, with my terrible memories of growing up with her. Every emotional button was being pushed by the mere thought of life under the same roof as her.

Despite my efforts to dissuade her, the following week Mom was at my door with two suitcases packed with everything she now owned. Before leaving Miami, everything else belonging to our family was placed in storage. My brothers and I never saw any of it again: a lifetime of mementos, like school diplomas, academic awards, jewelry, personal and family keepsakes and photos, was gone for good. Not a single personal item remained. In short, everything we had left behind as each of us left home had gone up in smoke along with our mother's mind. Everything got confiscated when she couldn't pay the storage bill.

There we were in San Antonio, she, a homeless, mentally ill forty-six-year-old, and me, a frightened twenty-four-year-old. It didn't take long to imagine a game plan as I sought an escape route for myself: I would have her arrested for trespassing and one of the city's social services agencies would figure out what to do with her. Then, I would also get my company to transfer me back to Kansas City where I would try to save my relationship with Maria. I gave no thought to what would eventually become of my mother.

I also gave little thought to my San Antonio-based girlfriend. Unfortunately, she would become collateral damage like other women before and after her did. My only concern right then was getting myself resituated hundreds of miles away from my mother.

In the end, I realized I could not just abandon my mother in San Antonio by moving back to Kansas City without her while she was in the custody of authorities. That would have been too cold a scheme even for me. Fortunately, my brother Mitch agreed to temporarily give Mom a place to sleep in his apartment in Lawrence.

Thank God for Mitch. That would give me some breathing space. I drove her to Kansas where we did the handoff. He brought her to his apartment where he introduced his disheveled and panicked mother to his shocked college roommates.

Mitch quickly decided on the same plan I had a few weeks earlier. Two weeks after she had arrived, the police came for her during dinner. He had her arrested for trespassing, domestic violence, or some other charge. She left quietly with them but was extremely upset.

Years later, Mitch told me that one of his roommates was even more upset. It took a while for him to recover from the experience of witnessing the delusional mother of his roommate being hauled off by the cops.

Our mother was placed in jail for her own safety and eventually moved to a city operated home for indigents. After evacuating Miami and then being rejected by her eldest son in San Antonio, shipped off to Kansas involuntarily, and finally, thrown in jail by another son all within a few weeks, Mom was shell-shocked. But I was, once again, happy. Within weeks, I was back in Kansas City doing my old job. Just an hour up the road from Lawrence, I told her I'd visit once in a while.

A few months later, I began looking for cheap accommodations in Kansas City where a social services agency could monitor her, still feeling guilty about the unfairness of having unloaded her on Mitch. Eventually, he and I found her government-subsidized Section 8 housing a couple of miles from my apartment. At about that time, Maria and I reconciled, although our relationship would not last.

13 Cool Jazz, Jet Setting, and Prayer

If music be the food of love, play on,
Give me excess of it; that surfeiting,
The appetite may sicken, and so die.

—WILLIAM SHAKESPEARE

Name: Robert
Age: 81
Diagnosis: Parkinson's senile degeneration of the brain

Soon into my first visit with Robert and his wife, Shelly, I knew this would be a different experience. When I entered his room, I told him what style of music I play and then asked if he was familiar with any of it. He quickly said he didn't "give a shit" if he recognized any of the songs I played. "Just play!" (The perfect audience.) Robert and Shelly were very cool people. We talked, laughed, and discussed types of music at length. They lived between Kansas City and the Upper East Side of Manhattan for a number of years when he was a top executive with a national construction company, traveling back and forth weekly. They were once true movers and shakers. Apparently, their New York

City neighbors included Donald Sutherland, Robert Redford, and Paul and Joan Newman.

Robert was a real Sinatra fan. We listened to "My Way" on YouTube during my first visit and sang together.

My second visit with Robert, two months later, was very productive in terms of patient engagement and mood. When I arrived, he was kind of slumped over in his wheelchair out in the hallway. He told me he was having a bad day and seemed lethargic and depressed. I played guitar and we also listened to some of his favorite artists on my smartphone—Frank Sinatra, Nat King Cole, Dean Martin, and Michael Bublé. I had just purchased a new portable speaker and it created a terrific bedside listening experience for him and everyone around us. Other patients and the staff were continuously stopping by his room to listen.

My third visit was spent streaming West Coast jazz, a late 1950's subgenre—the "cool jazz" of that era. This was Robert and Shelly's favorite music, featuring songs from artists like Stan Getz, Dave Brubeck, and Chico Hamilton. He and I talked and laughed a lot that day. Before I departed, Shelly showed up. They shared personal stories with me, and I shared a few with them, and Robert was clapping his hands to the music. They expressed much gratefulness for the visit and asked me to return.

Shelly was present during three of my visits. For each of them, she had baked fresh cookies for all of us and usually sat next to Robert's bedside or wheelchair holding his hand. Married when they were in their early twenties, she consistently praised him for the long fine life they had lived together. He loved hearing it.

Robert was the most grateful patient I've ever seen. He always told me how much he missed me and how he loved our musical visits. By my fourth visit, he had clearly deteriorated. At that time, I also found out that he and his wife were Christian

Scientists. Central to their beliefs is that Christian Science prayer is most effective when not combined with medicine. Thus, Robert chose prayer by itself as his exclusive treatment. I had not known how much pain he had endured until then because his upbeat nature and strong faith seemed to temper his discomfort.

Robert died soon after our fourth visit.

There are many instances where I've played for a client where their spouse is also present, enjoying the music with them. Sometimes the music appears to bring them closer together. Often, these marriages span a half-century or more, many beginning their courtship when they were just teenagers or in their early twenties. At times, I can't help but wonder what my own life might have looked like had I been emotionally stable and met my wife in my twenties, and we'd started our family sooner. Instead, I created mostly heartbreak and emotional scars during those years.

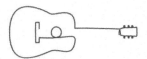

AFTER RETURNING FROM SAN ANTONIO, my next career move would take me closer to music. I was lucky to have returned to Kansas City with a job at my same company, but quickly became bored walking the floor of a retail store. A friend of mine, an old college roommate, suggested I apply to work for a rock radio station that had an opening for an advertising salesperson. That sounded very cool. I applied, got the job, and cleaned myself up. Wearing suits and ties, I tried on the role of being a sales executive in an exciting industry. Best of all, I was in an environment where I was around music all the time, hanging out with the disc jockeys, meeting celebrity artists when they were in town to do on-air interviews to promote their shows. I got free concert tickets and began learning the broadcasting business. My income had more than doubled.

Over the next few years, I changed radio stations a handful of times, with every move just about doubling my income. At last, I had found a profession.

Maria and I had an on-again, off-again relationship for a few years. We were never the same after my San Antonio separation. We tried living together three different times, each of us taking turns leaving the other behind in order to "explore." We loved each other yet loved our personal freedom even more. It was she who finally had the courage to engage us in the DTR talk. That's short for *Define the Relationship*. This is the big, serious discussion that smart couples have at some point to establish a mutual understanding of their status as a couple.

In the case of Maria and myself, the big question on the table was: Do we just continue bouncing back and forth between being committed and uncommitted, existing in an open relationship? What might a future like this look like?

The hardest part of such a talk is being vulnerable enough to be honest with the other person. If one partner expresses feelings about wanting a relationship that is understood to be a permanent, exclusive arrangement, there's the danger that the other partner might not feel the same way. Neither of us had the guts to say that. Our DTR talk did not contain the word *marriage.*

Maria and I had now been together about five years. Thus, the talk was very late in the game for us. We were each carrying enough emotional baggage to sink a ship. What I realized later was that Maria had already figured this out and was starting to bond with someone else. She was about to make a choice but was afraid to tell me without first getting a sense of where I stood. I was simply too obtuse to understand how revealing our talk would be for her. I was relieved at the end when she said, "I love you," and went home.

Our DTR talk was about two weeks prior to her birthday and I wanted to do something special for her. A normal person probably would have given the woman he loved chocolates, flowers, or jewelry or thrown her a party. But not me. It just didn't cross my mind.

I could've written a note expressing my appreciation for our recent talk and taken her to dinner. But because Maria had recently struggled with some back pain, I gave her a heating pad and a Hallmark card with my signature as the only personalized expression of my feelings for her on her special day. Upon receiving these, she smiled and said thanks.

A few weeks later, Maria told me she had found someone else. When I asked how this had happened, she gave no answer other than to say in a tone of resignation, "Steve, you can't be intimate." I didn't even know what the word *intimate* meant, so this remark left me silenced.

Later that week, I went to a bookstore and purchased a book about intimacy in the self-help section. I recall losing interest in it after the first couple of chapters. Most of it made little sense and didn't seem to apply to me.

My response to losing Maria was about four weeks of deep sadness, large doses of cocaine and alcohol, and solitude with my guitar. Afterward, I quickly went on the hunt for new love to numb my pain.

In Shakespeare's *Twelfth Night,* the play's opening speech and overall theme might as well be an ode to my personal life throughout my twenties. The unhappy, lovesick main character in the play tells his musicians, "If music be the food of love, play on." Soon after, he asks them to give him so much musical passion-food that he will overdose and cease to desire love any longer. In other words, he's aware he might choke on too much of a good thing and then starve the love out of a relationship.

For me, this line is an image of disordered love, something both wanted and unwanted among some people. The play raises the question of whether romantic love has more to do with the reality of the person who is loved or with their imagination. Between nineteen and twenty-nine, I had three long-term relationships—supposedly committed. These lasted four, five, and two years, respectively. Each directly followed the preceding one, with little or no space between them. Throughout this period, I probably had north of thirty additional love interests on the side. All these were betrayals, either one-night stands or short-lived affairs.

Throughout my twenties, like Duke Orsino, the main character of the play, I was in love with the idea of being in love. I embraced the idea of a long-term committed relationship but couldn't get through the ordinary routines that all couples fall into which might lead to a permanent future. I simply couldn't imagine what that might look like. In my supposed long-term relationships, I thought I was settled in with each woman for years. Then, a strange twist on this dynamic would occur. Suddenly, I'd switch lovers at a moment's notice, but would do so only on a trial basis.

First, I'd meet some new object of my desire and begin fantasizing about her. I'd find myself romancing the new woman until she appeared to want me. If she didn't, I would move on to another prospect. Ultimately, however, I wasn't willing to take the chance of failure with any of them, leaving me with no one. And so, I wouldn't tell my existing girlfriend, thinking I'd have the safety of the current long-term relationship as a fallback.

This was not a conscious strategy.

There could only be two outcomes: I would be successful in my new pursuit and eventually end the old relationship, or the old girlfriend would discover my unfaithfulness, break up with me, or begin cheating also, ultimately moving on to more fertile ground.

A cycle of temporary stability mixed with an ongoing search for a more exciting adventure never had a happy ending. It would just keep repeating itself. This dynamic is not unusual for young people who are discovering themselves as they explore relationships. Most, however, learn the grass is not always greener elsewhere. Also, they are not always dishonest with a longtime lover when they decide to move on with another flame. At some point, one makes a conscious decision not to be seduced by the fantasy of a new relationship and thus avoid a costly emotional mistake.

For me, hit-and-run hookups became standard operating procedure. I had not yet learned that the grass is only greener where its watered.

14 Tuesdays with Owen

*Without music to decorate it, time is just a bunch of boring
production deadlines or dates by which bills must be paid.*

—FRANK ZAPPA

Name: Owen
Age: 83
Diagnosis: Acute respiratory failure

I made more musical visits to Owen than to any other patient.
We were scheduled every Tuesday for around three months. He
was usually in his wheelchair and always alert and glad to see
me. Each time I visited, he was watching old westerns on his in-
room TV, shows like *Gunsmoke* and *Bonanza.* Our first visit was
terrific. He sang along with tunes he knew. During my second
visit, however, he seemed a bit bored. Maybe he was tiring of my
playing style or my choice of songs.

When I asked Owen what kind of music and which artists he
liked. He said, "Waylon Jennings." If you are familiar with this
artist, then you might know that Waylon Jennings is part of a
subgenre of American country music known as *outlaw country,*
somewhat popular in the 1970s and early 1980s. Other well-

known "outlaws" are Willie Nelson, Kris Kristofferson, and Jerry Jeff Walker. These artists were industry outlaws, refusing to work according to the establish norms of the recording industry. Refusing standard expectations that they create highly produced, slick studio works, they insisted that their recordings sound raw, like their in-person playing in bars and small venues. Mistakes, glitches, and all were to be part of that package. Neither did they dress or act like big country music stars. Their previously slick "Nashville sound" soon became known as the "Austin" sound. Texas became home base.

On my next visit, I returned with a surprise. I took out my phone, opened the music app, and typed in Owen's favorite artist. For the next sixty minutes, I streamed Waylon Jennings' greatest hits on a small external speaker I carry with me. Owen recognized most of the songs. At times, he would just lean his head back in his wheelchair, stare at the ceiling, and drift off in his own thoughts. During some songs, there were tears in his eyes. I assumed these songs triggered happy feelings and memories.

That particular session happened to coincide with lunch at the nursing home. When an orderly came into the room to let Owen know that his favorite dish, baked spaghetti, was being served in the dining room, Owen told her to "forget it." He said that he wasn't leaving the room! Whatever the music triggered in him was pretty powerful.

For weeks, we listened to the same outlaw country music artists. I never again brought my guitar when visiting Owen. I had become a digital music companion rather than a musician. Listening together added a different dimension to the experience. While live music is a special gift, I quickly realized that anyone could stream music. You don't have to be a musician to do this. In the digital age, just about any musical taste can be accommodated on the fly.

Owen died after I'd made about a dozen weekly visits.

When a patient wants to hear the same songs over and over again during the course of many visits, that makes it easy on a bedside musician, especially when the music is being streamed—no more hunting for new music for each session. However, the repetitiveness of hearing the same songs and artists over many weeks can become a thoughtless endeavor, and in the case of Owen, led to my regularly drifting off into my own thoughts, forgetting that this was to be a shared volunteer-client experience. All that late Seventies and early Eighties outlaw music took me back to one of the most painful times in my own life.

Ultimately, being a serial monogamist and cheater blew up in my face. I had become a relationship "outlaw" chasing female outlaws. I was twenty-eight when I found myself in a therapist's chair to manage the explosion, which is where I discovered that women who were warm and affectionate were often attracted to me although I lacked the inner wherewithal to reciprocate if they got too close. My own instincts led me to women who were distant, detached, and not particularly affectionate except when it came to sex. It was startling to realize they were much like myself. The colder they were, the more I was attracted to them. It made no sense.

Two years earlier, when Maria called it quits on our five-year relationship, it took less than a month for me to get attached to someone who I met in a bar. Within a few weeks, we were inseparable. Friends were mystified by how quickly I had leaped into a new relationship. Jill was a social worker with her own troubled history of broken relationships. She was emotionally shallow, unaffectionate, and a chronic complainer. She'd send me into fits of agitation when she whined about one thing or another, especially about problems that I thought she had imagined. Nevertheless, I was crazy for her. However, after a couple of years, this woman became so frustrated with my lack of empathy and my inability to allow her to vent that she eventually ended our relationship, sending me into a tailspin. This was the relationship that motivated me to begin work with a therapist to figure out what was wrong with me.

Over years of therapy, I slowly recognized that I had trained myself as a child to tune out the nonstop delusional histrionics— over issues both small and large—that my mother's disordered mind had manufactured. At times, I thought her delusions were directed at me; I'd supposedly done something wrong and was being threatened with punishment. My child brain interpreted these scenarios as pending violence. This kind of thing came with the schizophrenic territory my brothers and I were living in.

My adult brain responded the same way: Whenever a significant woman in my life would become emotionally upset or seemingly irrational, I'd respond as if I were being attacked even though the outburst would have nothing to do with me. My hair-trigger response would be to attack back, leaving the woman in shock. Jill's complaints were triggering events.

Back in childhood, tuning my mom out or lashing out at the slightest hint of an oncoming episode had turned into a self-protective defense mechanism that was not very satisfying the older I got. In my mid-teens, I started to deploy an offensive strategy. I would "out-crazy" my mother with loud, aggressive verbal threats—although things usually didn't work out the way I hoped they would. With her agitation only heightened by my tactic, she'd sometimes sneak up behind me, beating my head with her fists as I tried to protect myself.

Mom would also commit worse acts. Often, a few days after these confrontations, I'd return home from school and discover that things in my bedroom were missing or destroyed. Posters of musicians I loved had been torn off the walls, trophies were shattered; their pieces tossed in a trashcan. Another instance of my mother's recklessness was the disappearance of a handwritten short story I had been working on. I was too discouraged to start over again.

The worst episode was my discovery of a pile of small broken pieces of wood on my desk. These had been my collection of miniature handmade guillotines. I had carefully designed the pieces, cutting them out of balsa wood and gluing them together. For the blade, I used a shaving razor blade, carefully cutting a groove on each upright so it would accurately drop and land in the right place. I had about a half-dozen of these. She hadn't even bothered to throw away the pieces after crushing them.

I recently recounted the guillotine episode to my therapist, and he broke out laughing. It took me a moment to catch on before I realized an amusing aspect of that story: a kid with a hobby of designing and building precision execution devices, instead of model cars, planes, and ships.

I don't recall ever hitting my mother back or confronting her over any of this behavior, but I did keep a baseball bat by my bedside in case of a nighttime intrusion.

Although I would not marry until I was age thirty-one and despite doing therapy for three years before marriage, these issues lingered. My wife, Cynthia, would have no small role in helping me understand that my childhood relationship with my mother was a continuous subplot running alongside the unfolding story of most of my primary female relationships, including with her. Over a period of years, she would repeatedly explain that I had irrationally projected some version of my mother in past female relationships and was continuing to do so with her.

My armed fortress of behaviors created a train wreck in the early years of our marriage. These would manifest as an inability to discriminate between the wide range of emotions she expressed. I certainly didn't yet possess the patience to listen if she was simply having a bad day. My hidden emotional subplot interpreted this as "unnecessary drama."

As with women from prior relationships, she felt I wasn't honoring her emotions. If she displayed even slight annoyance with me, I would verbally attack her. A simple conversation might escalate, therefore, into something ugly, leaving hurt feelings on both sides. The inheritance I received from my mother—or, as I think of it, the gift that keeps on giving—was this thick wall of defenses and combativeness. As with many children of a parent who has schizophrenia, it would be one of the ongoing challenges of my life to recognize these behaviors, unravel them, and reprogram myself.

When my oldest grandson was about nine, he asked me about the bat I still keep by the side of the bed where his grandmother and I sleep. I told him it is there "to help keep out intruders."

15 Until Death Do Us Part

Music, once admitted to the soul, becomes a sort of spirit, and never dies.

—EDWARD BULWER-LYTTON

Sixteen clients
Age: 80–93
Diagnosis: Various

Around two-thirds of my client visits are with folks over the age of eighty. A majority of them are females. I don't know precisely how many are married when I see them, but through conversation, I estimate the figure is pretty low, mostly due to the death of their spouses. Still married or not, many had achieved fifty or more years of marriage. I sometimes ask what they discovered along the way to a long marriage. They say:

"Fifteen percent of conflict is difference of opinion. Eighty-five percent is tone of voice."

"Apologizing doesn't always mean you're wrong and the other is right. It means you value the relationship more than your ego."

"Imagine what your life would really be without them."

"A hug and a kiss go a long way."

"Do stuff together, like going to the grocery store. Every date doesn't have to include expensive or exciting outings. Small errands can remind you that just each other's company can be fun."

"Laugh at yourself and at each other."

"The grass is never greener. Whatever your problems, you'll likely take them with you."

"I'm not Cinderella and he's not Prince Charming."

"Always kiss each other goodnight."

"Marriage is a team sport. You can only win by playing together."

"Keep doing the same things you did while you were falling in love. They probably have something to do with what got you to the altar."

"Create space for yourself. Take a break but don't say goodbye."

"Keep creating new memories. Travel together, go somewhere and just have fun."

"Once in a while, do at least one thing that you may not like but that thrills the other. If she loves to dance but you don't, surprise her once in a while. If he loves cars but you find them boring, take him to a car show."

"Do service work together. We volunteered for causes for which we both feel deeply, like working a soup kitchen and at animal shelters. Volunteering strengthened us as a couple."

"Observance of our faith. God had no small role in bringing us together and guided us as we grew old together."

Today, after thirty-five years of marriage, this advice makes so much sense. Much of it seems so obvious, almost too simple. Yet how many of us payed attention when we heard things like this while we were still dating our future spouses? How many of us exercise much of this wisdom well into our marriages? I would have saved myself and my wife, Cynthia, a lot of grief had I been more aware at the outset.

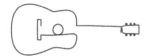

IN THE LATE 1970S AND EARLY 1980S, new technology and new media platforms began to alter how music was made and its delivery. At the beginning of that period, analog recording technology was at its zenith. The delivery of most home-recorded music was on vinyl discs, eight-track music players were in most cars, and cassette players, both in-dashboard and at home, were in the ascendant. For portability, there was the Sony Walkman®.

By 1982, eight-track tapes had become obsolete. Cassettes would hang on for just a few more years. The number of FM radio stations began multiplying, splintering into dozens of new music formats. Instead of just a handful of FM radio formats in most cities, there would end up being twenty-five or more. Each would provide a specialized format for different tastes: soft rock, classic rock, heavy metal rock, contemporary pop; R&B, gospel, urban contemporary, and hip-hop, among others. Where there had been one country music station, there would now be three or more, each appealing to a different segment of the country music audience. AM radio with its inferior fidelity was forced to evolve into varieties of news, talk, and sports programs.

In 1982, the first CD players came to market, ushering in the mass-market digital age in purchased music, which was the precursor of downloadable MP3 files.

Television also splintered at the same time—again having a profound effect on music. In 1977, most people could watch just three to five local broadcast TV channels and there was just one national cable network. By 1980, there was CNN, ESPN, and dozens more networks about to launch. In 1981, music had found its own TV network. MTV (Music Television) launched with the Buggles' song "Video Killed the Radio Star." This was the first music video to air on the new cable television channel. MTV posed an existential threat to the radio industry, offering greater exposure to new artists.

And then there was the trending music itself. Disco, an entire cultural movement fueled by a single genre of music, was ubiquitous. With an explosion in the number of radio and specialized TV channels, families no longer sat around the same TV set, watching the same shows together, as they had since the earliest days of television. Beginning in the 1980s, family members began watching programs unique to their individual tastes on separate television sets in different rooms of the home. Music lovers were thrilled. The culture was moving in every direction at once and there were more great songs than anyone could count.

Some of the music from this period became my memory markers for both major and small inconsequential events. My guitar playing had been growing stale for years from lack of practice and inspiration, but I was fully engaged with the music world as it was vitalized by new technology as a result of being in the radio business. My memories are reflected back through some of the biggest radio airplay hits of that era like:

- "Hotel California," The Eagles
- "Rich Girl," Hall & Oates
- "Best of My Love," The Emotions
- "Carry On Wayward Son," Kansas

- "Miss You," The Rolling Stones
- "Dust in the Wind," Kansas
- "September," Earth, Wind & Fire
- "Double Vision," Foreigner
- "Le Freak," Chic
- "What a Fool Believes," Doobie Brothers
- "After the Love Is Gone," Earth, Wind & Fire
- "Babe," Styx
- "Another Brick in the Wall," Pink Floyd
- "Crazy Little Thing Called Love," Queen
- "Tainted Love," Soft Cell
- "Don't Stand So Close to Me," The Police
- "Kiss on My List," Hall & Oates
- "Africa," Toto
- "Every Breath You Take," The Police
- "Sexual Healing," Marvin Gaye

There's no telling why some songs stick while others don't. Many were not my favorites, but I nevertheless have vivid associations with them, like the disco hit "Le Freak." Although I disliked disco music, it was a dominant style of the era and was played nonstop in gay bars. After observing that straight women would go to these places to dance without getting hit on by guys, I came up with what I thought to be a clever scheme. Going to these dance emporiums by myself, I'd get girls to dance with me and engage in conversation. Who knew what that might lead to?

It only resulted in getting my ass pinched by men as they handed me their phone numbers, trying to pick me up.

Foreigner's album *Double Vision* was released the month prior to the start of my career in radio. The title song is the first song I can recall hearing at work on my first day on the job as an advertising salesperson. Played constantly everywhere, it became a permanently imprinted trigger. That hard-charging hit is still played on classic rock radio stations everywhere to this day.

For me, the song "Double Vision" reflects the joyous beginning of my professional life; an aggressive young guy with no place to go but into his future. Even as an older man now, the song still gives me a rush of youthful optimism.

Today, the song "Sexual Healing" brings back a single memory that makes me smile. Cynthia and I were about to go on our first date. I came to her apartment and she asked me to wait in her living room while she finished getting ready. Before going to her bedroom, she put Marvin Gaye's *Midnight Love* album on her stereo. When "Sexual Healing" played, I recall thinking to myself that there was no way she would be sending me a message like that at the outset of our first date.

She wasn't.

16 The Artist, Entrepreneur, and Hustler

ARTHUR "BLIND" BLAKE, "CHUMP MAN BLUES," 1929

Name: Betty
Age: 100
Diagnosis: Lung cancer

Betty, who had just celebrated her one hundredth birthday, lived in a small apartment in an assisted living community. As I approached her front door, I noticed a large metal street sign, hand-painted in colorful letters on it that read: Betty Boop-Oop-A-Doop!

I thought, *Cute! That's probably the work of one of her grandkids or great grandkids.* Then I knocked and heard a melodic voice sing out in response, "Come innn . . ." Even before entering, I could tell it was meant as a warm humorous greeting.

I walked into the den and saw Betty sitting there smiling in an overstuffed chair. I said, "Hi, I'm Steve, a volunteer. I was invited here to play music for you. Did anyone tell you I was coming? I brought my guitar."

Betty quickly cut me off, saying, "I know you brought a guitar. That thing in your hands is certainly not a piano or a dishwasher!" She then smiled and let me know she was delighted that I was there. As I looked for a place to sit with my guitar, I scanned her cluttered apartment. It had a small kitchen, meaning she was capable of cooking for herself. On the floor—albeit leaning against all four walls—were TV trays painted with colorful floral designs, maybe as many as fifteen to twenty of them. A number of the trays also had the Betty Boop cartoon character painted on them in a variety of poses.

There were floor-to-ceiling shelves filled with books and small craft objects. More books were piled high on tables along with some unfinished pencil drawings. On the walls were framed paintings and elaborate needle point images—all of them her personal creations.

Apparently, Betty was watching me closely. "It is all for sale," she said.

I glibly replied by asking if she was having an estate sale. She found humor in this remark, which I had not intended, and quickly responded, "Oh no! Estate sales are for people who are leaving permanently. I'm not going anywhere. Selling my art and books is a nice little sideline business that puts a few bucks in my pocket. Besides, I'm too lazy to clean up the place so I'm always having a sale."

She told me she painted the trays herself and did all the crafts too. These were little sculptures of elves and animals. She said she had also painted the Betty Boop sign over her front door. After she let me look around a bit more, she said, "I can give you twenty percent off today." I didn't know if she was just being funny or actually offering me a sweet deal before I lost interest. I told her I'd think on it.

We talked a bit and then I played my first song. It was "Chump Man Blues," the funny 1920's Blind Blake song about a guy whose wife is always mad at him, treats him mean and driving him to despair. He complains throughout the song that she's turned him into a chump, but he loves her too much to leave. Like most of the female clients I've played this for, Betty thought it was one of the funniest songs she'd ever heard.

Next up was her request for some barbershop quartet music. I'd never had such a request before and told her that it required many singers and that the songs were usually sung a cappella with no musical accompaniment. She might as well have asked me to sing opera. She said, "It's no problem, I'll do it alone." And she did!

It turned out, she had been a member of the local chapter of Sweet Adelines, an international organization of women who perform barbershop quartet-style songs at assisted living facilities and nursing homes. Betty sang two songs solo, both classics: "It Had to Be You" and "After You've Gone." Her singing was surprisingly good.

While listening, I looked at some framed photographs. The pictures had people wearing clothing from the era of 1930s to 1940s. I asked about them and she said that while living in Los Angeles in the 1930s, she'd dress up with friends and drive around in her Model-A Ford. She explained, "That's what everyone did in those days. We'd put on some nice driving clothes and go for a spin."

After about an hour together, I told Betty it was time for me to leave, as my wife was expecting me home to take care of some errands. She quickly responded, saying, "You'd better leave quickly, or you might be singing the Chump Man blues tonight!"

I chuckled and as I walked toward the door, Betty handed me a business card. It was for her daughter, a psychotherapist. She said if I ever needed some counseling her daughter might as well get my business. I smiled and thanked her.

Before I stepped out of the apartment, she called me back and handed me a four-color printout of her collection of hand-painted holiday greeting cards, offering me a box of ten for only $14. I barely escaped with my wallet in my pocket.

Every musical visit is unique, depending on each client's personality, age, and diagnosis, as well as how advanced their condition was and their current mood. These variables impact the degree to which they engage with me. Nevertheless, there were times when I thought I had experienced almost every possible situation until I met Betty.

In Betty's case, there was another variable: mental acuity. Her sharpness of mind. The term *mental acuity* takes into consideration the ability to focus, memory, concentration, and understanding. It's not a measurement of intelligence. It's also not related to performing complex functions or even to remembering what has been learned over a lifetime. It is a measure of how well or poorly the brain is functioning.

With someone of Betty's age and lifetime experiences, one gets a different perspective about the passage of time and how much can be experienced in a hundred years. For instance, Betty had two marriages, each longer than mine is yet—and I've already been married to the same woman for over thirty-five years.

It's often said that successful marriages are the outcome of work and perseverance. For our marriage, it took that and more. It was a triumph of hope over experience. I also believe there have been periodic divine interventions to guide and assist us along the way.

When Cynthia and I met, I was working at KSAS, a Kansas City classic rock station. This was my third radio station job in as many years, each one an advancement. While my personal life was often in turmoil, my professional life was steadily advancing. I had just been promoted to sales manager when we were introduced at a business lunch.

Cynthia was the director of advertising for a big, regional concert promotion company. She was one of the largest buyers of radio advertising in the market. In the local radio world, she was a queen, spending millions of dollars a year promoting big-name music acts in regional concert halls and arenas, artists like Bob Seeger, Bette Midler, the Eagles, James Taylor, Michael Jackson, Rick Springfield, Joni Mitchell, Stevie Ray Vaughn, the Grateful Dead, Bruce Springsteen, the Rolling Stones, the Oak Ridge Boys, and Tom Petty and the Heartbreakers. As a rock radio station playing most of these artists, the KSAS audience was a natural fit for her marketing. She had lots of money to spend and concert tickets to hand out as favors. Everyone in the radio business was her friend.

Our first business lunch was not memorable. The conversation centered mainly on how my radio station could help her sell more tickets to shows. What got my attention took place a few days later when she stopped by the radio station just to say hello. I don't recall much of our conversation that day because I was distracted by her looks. Music may be a powerful trigger of old memories, but I don't need a song to recall every detail of her appearance. From head to toe, she was beautiful and had style. Tall and slender, she wore a rose-colored beret. Her coat was a chocolate-brown corduroy at mid-calf length with a shawl collar and a tie belt. From the beret to her black, knee-high leather boots, she was perfect. And what a set of legs!

Who actually remembers those kinds of details years later? Someone who was smitten.

She told me later that she had come by to flirt.

We soon arranged another business lunch, even though it was unnecessary. We liked one another from the start but quickly learned we each already had a main relationship underway with someone else. Any ideas about dating were fleeting.

Besides, dating a client is a risky proposition, especially if they are one of your largest customers. There is an inherent imbalance of power when one party to a relationship is a major source of revenue for the other. If the love goes south, so might your income.

I would learn much later that the only thing more dangerous is when two people at the same company date and one reports to the other. Talk about an imbalance of power! In that case, a breakup can lead to a lawsuit from the subordinate.

On the surface, Cynthia and I were a classic example of the adage "opposites attract." We were from different worlds in both small and large ways; I came from the urban Northeast, was an agnostic with a secular Jewish background, and she was a nonpracticing Catholic from a devoutly religious family of farmers, ranchers, and mechanics in rural South Dakota. She had dozens of cousins and knew them all. I was too embarrassed to admit that I had no relationship with any of mine—in fact, that I didn't even know most of their names.

Cynthia was an intellectual who probably read two or three books a week. Me, two or three per year. I lived in an old regentrified part of the city, she in the newer suburbs. Her comfort food of choice was an open roast beef sandwich with mashed potatoes and gravy. Mine, Chicken Tikka Masala with a side of chickpea curry. She was not a user of drugs, not even pot. Both below and above the surface, we seemed to be polar opposites. She seemed so warm and normal without any apparent issues, not edgy, quirky, or slightly distant like other women I had been attracted to. She was straight as an arrow— or so I thought at the time.

Our occasional meetings ended when I took a job at another radio station and there was no longer a pretense for getting together. More than a year would pass before we saw each other again. Cynthia was at my new radio station's production studio creating radio commercials for an upcoming concert. One of my colleagues handled her account and was showing her around our offices. That's when we bumped into each other. We spontaneously embraced like old friends at a reunion. One week later, we had our first date. I was recovering from my relationship going up in flames a few months earlier and hers was about to end. The way was now clear.

Picking her up at her apartment and not wanting to appear too eager to impress, I drove us to a small, rundown Asian restaurant in an equally rundown part of the city. I had shared in advance that we were going to a small Chinese joint, unlike the big, nice family establishments in the suburbs. When we arrived, the place had a neon sign in the window that read CHINESE SOUL FOOD. We had landed at the culinary intersection of Szechuan and American Southern-fried cooking. Today, such a place is described as a fusion concept. This would be perfect for a laugh and a gauge of how far her food tastes stretched.

I don't remember the exact dishes we ordered for dinner that evening, but they were probably something like fried rice and pork neck bones with a side of bok choy or collard greens. She found it interesting, though not a meal she would soon repeat. During dinner, Cynthia thought that a light conversation about one of her favorite subjects might interest me. Unfolding a cocktail napkin, she drew a bell curve model, asking me if I knew what it was. I said I thought so, and she then explained that it had to do with probability distribution, that a bell curve can accurately describe the distribution of data within a given population.

As an example, with correctly input data, you can graph the size of the population with an average IQ, the slopes representing the part that is below average and the part that are geniuses. The middle was where the majority of the population resided.

I found her actual example to be odd. It was the idea that the distribution of spiritual consciousness among the general population might also be illustrated by using a bell curve. On the left side of the curve were folks with no soul awareness. The large middle, representing people with varying levels of spiritual awareness is the top of the bell curve. The downward slope on the right side of the curve represents the small number of highly aware mystics among us. By the time she got to that point, my eyes may have glazed over, as I was wondering how anyone might capture the input data to create such a chart.

After dinner, we went to hear some music at the Total Experience Lounge, a blues bar frequented almost exclusively by Black folks. I wanted to surprise her with a musical experience she had probably never had, even as a concert promoter. I watched her expression as we drove deep into a part of the city where she had never previously ventured. She was wide-eyed but showed no sign of concern. She shared that she had only known one Black person growing up in South Dakota. I was surprised when we both got frisked for weapons at the door, she was mostly amused. We were the only White folks among over one hundred people, and she danced with every guy who asked, while I just observed. We still laugh about one older man who suggested we watch others on the dance floor, because: "You have no rhythm in you."

17 Betty Boop Philosophy

Well it goes to St. Louis
Down to Missouri
Oklahoma City looks oh so pretty
You'll see Amarillo
Gallup, New Mexico
Flagstaff, Arizona
Don't forget Wynonna
Kingman, Barstow, San Bernardino

Won't you get hip to this kindly tip
And go take that California trip
Get your kicks on Route 66

—BOB TROUP, "(GET YOUR KICKS ON) ROUTE 66," 1957

Name: Betty
Age: 100
Diagnosis: Lung cancer

This would be my second visit with Betty. I had seen her just six weeks earlier. When asked to see her again, I was told she had been moved to another unit at the facility. Initially, she had been in the independent living section, long before she was diagnosed with lung cancer. There she'd had an apartment with a full kitchen, living room, and separate bedroom, large enough to display her many art projects, where she could easily entertain visitors.

Betty now resided in the assisted-living wing. Her new unit was just one room with a bed, two stuffed chairs, a TV, and a few other small pieces of furniture. There was no kitchen. No longer cooking for herself, she joined others for meals in a central dining hall.

The hand-painted Betty Boop street sign had been hung inside her new room. Noticing there was not enough wall space to display most of her other paintings, I asked what happened to them. She said she'd talked the staff into displaying some of her artwork in the building's main lobby by the visitor entrance. She had cut a deal where she'd give them a split of the sale price on anything they sold on her behalf. "A consignment arrangement," she told me. She also suggested that before I exit the building, I should look over her pieces and then see her directly to get a "friends and family deal."

If Betty's condition had gotten worse, it was not at all evident. She had requested I come back and was happy to see me. She quickly wanted to get on with the musical part of our visit. However, I never took out my guitar. She knew all about music streaming, which I found unusual for a person of her age, so I suggested a game, she would pick a category of music and I would search within it and stream a song through my phone.

Her first category was "cheek-to-cheek" songs. Not knowing what that was meant, she told me, "Songs for slow dancing." As an example, she told me to find "Stardust" by Nat King Cole. After that, I thought I'd surprise her with others like "The Very Thought of You" by Etta James, "Blue Moon," and "As Time Goes

By." They were all classics. She knew the lyrics to all of them and sang each song with conviction.

After a while, Betty took out a photo album and shared a picture taken of her in LA's Chinatown district in 1940. I asked her when she had moved there. She proudly told me that in 1939, at age nineteen, she and her husband whom she had met just months earlier, packed up their old Model A Ford, leaving Wichita and catching Route 66 in Oklahoma City all the way to California. They had just $60 in their pockets.

We talked for a while and then I asked what the most exciting period of her life was. She said it was during Prohibition, a period when she spent boozing it up in speakeasies. These she explained were illegal bars that sold liquor, often operated by organized crime. It was then that I suspected Betty might be losing her memory. She probably never stepped foot in a speakeasy—she would have been too young. Prohibition ended in the early 1930s.

Before I said goodbye, I asked her the most important advice she might share from her hundred years of life. She quickly replied, "Make lots of plans for everything you want to do and then "go with the flow and expect nothing." She then suggested we stream one last song and chose, "(Get Your Kicks on) Route 66."

Betty passed away about two months later, on Christmas Day.

Reflecting on how teenage Betty and her husband started their life together, I compared it with how Cynthia and I started ours. Our big adventures were occasional two-hour drives to her parent's farm. I was thirty and she twenty-nine. In the weeks following our first date, we became best friends. Almost all our free time was spent together, although, by my choice, there was no expression of romance. The big move in that direction was my gently taking her hand at a dinner party after a couple of months. We had exchanged not even a kiss up to then. That took another few weeks.

One evening, Cynthia finally asked me why I wasn't more assertive. I gave her some excuse, but the truth was that I was unraveling inside. I knew where we were headed and, knowing my history, it scared me. I felt my vulnerability for the first time in my life. Perhaps I had never felt this way with other women because I never found myself interested in those who were as warm and open as Cynthia. Or perhaps the truth of it was that I felt unsafe. I simply had never allowed most of those earlier relationships to progress very far.

Despite my compatibility with Cynthia, at some level I was afraid that I would be exposed as an inept, frightened person and would ultimately be rejected for it. These are the sorts of buried feelings that are commonly possessed by a child raised by a parent who has schizophrenia. These feelings slowly surface once they begin digging into their past while trying to intimately engage with another person. Past feelings of inadequacy and the defense mechanisms that have kept them hidden impose themselves once these people enter new relationships.

One of the ways I had avoided revealing myself to others throughout my youth was to hide my past from myself. This was accomplished by a trick the mind plays on people who have experienced deep trauma. Memories are blocked. That way the trauma and the environment in which it took place won't easily be reexperienced. As a defensive mechanism, I had lost almost all memories prior to the age of thirteen. There was an occasional fleeting recollection of some events, but few of these memories were positive, and none included my mother or father engaged in any constructive activities with me. I had not a single memory of our entire family together, not even at the dinner table. In my memories of myself, I was always alone.

The closer Cynthia and I got, the more frequently I'd feel out of control. I began to cancel dates with little notice, preferring to stay at home alone with a fifth of vodka and a gram of cocaine. Every time though, I'd call her late during the evening of the cancelled date. Head buzzing and drunk, I'd apologize and ask if we could talk. She would patiently listen and engage with me. Knowing I was seeing a therapist, she even agreed to join us at a session at his request. He was trying to help both of us get through my fear of intimacy. Naturally, as the subject of my mother kept coming up, Cynthia slowly became aware of what she was getting into.

My mother was now in her fifties and her symptoms had stabilized. This was the second-best outcome for someone like her. About a third of schizophrenia patients are actually considered cured if they can move beyond the symptoms, perhaps having been initially misdiagnosed. Another third deteriorates. My mother was among the third who would eventually stabilize. Medicated with sedatives, she was trapped in her little apartment, getting out only when a social services agency volunteer came to take her to the supermarket or her doctor.

Although schizophrenia is not a disorder that can be reversed, its symptoms can be managed. As my mother accepted her need for drugs, the hallucinations began to subside, and her delusions became less intense. Even so, I could only bring myself to see her once every couple of months and only for brief periods. I would hold my breath knowing that a visit was just around the corner and would be agitated for hours after leaving.

After these visits I felt bad about myself for feeling as I did. I still resented her for being sick and blamed her for my guilt about not taking care of her. Cynthia, on the other hand, was the first woman I dated to invite herself to join me on these visits.

She was always kind, patient, and compassionate. I gave her little credit for her patience with my mother though, telling myself it's easy to be that way with someone who didn't torment you as a child.

Knowing at a rational level that my mother suffered from a debilitating illness and was not responsible for her behaviors did not reduce my bitterness. My deep-seated pain and anger completely extinguished any notion of compassion or forgiveness.

18 The Family Who Knew How to Say Goodbye

A painter paints pictures on canvas.
But musicians paint their pictures on silence.

—LEOPOLD STOKOWSKI

Name: Georgette
Age: 81
Diagnosis: Breast cancer

As a hospice volunteer, I am always learning the different things that are done to care for someone as they begin the final stages of dying, also known as *active dying.* This stage typically lasts about three days. Common to this stage are changes in consciousness and breathing, blood pressure dropping, minimal intake or output of food and liquids, extremities feeling cold to the touch, a numbness in the extremities, and with some, delirium.

Although I have not been present in the final moment of someone's life, I have on occasion been called to play music during the hours leading up to that time. For Georgette, it was an honor to be with family members who had begun a vigil. They were trying to comfort their mom and themselves at the same time. Because many of us have never gone through this process with a loved one or have only done so infrequently, most family members I meet seem unprepared. They are caught up in their grief or discomfort as the person they love passes. Often, they are quietly waiting and praying. In these moments, I softly strum chords on my guitar so as not to intrude on the moment. I will try to play some ambient music, songs that are nonmelodic, almost without a recognizable melody and meditative in nature, sort of dreamy.

When I entered Georgette's room, there were about seven family members there who had been visiting in shifts. Chaplain Bill, a staff member at the hospice, was also present and keeping watch over "Georgie," whom I was told was actively dying. Her impending death was possibly just hours away. "Any time now," her nurse told me.

Those present included her three adult kids, two of their spouses, and Georgie's ex-husband. He told me they were married for thirty-two years and divorced for twenty! He was crying as much as their kids over this woman who hadn't been his life partner in such a long time.

What I observed in that room was an experience that was both joyful and painful. The family told stories, held hands, laughed, and cried, knowing they were nearing the end and getting ready to say goodbye. They had done everything possible to prepare themselves and their mom for her transition. Most notably, they were not afraid.

They had tried to anticipate and orchestrate the experience with guidance and ideas from their hospice team about:

- Pain management. Hospice medical staff was there to provide timely pain medication for maximum comfort.

- The environment. Soft lighting, soft voices, no more than three or four people in the room at any time to avoid Georgie being overwhelmed. No background noise from any type of electronics or screen devices, other than the careful selection of music.
- Soothing acoustic music.
- Spiritual support from the hospice chaplain.
- Connection with a faraway relation. They video streamed an out-of-town relative who could not be there. She wanted to see and speak with Georgie, even though Georgie may not have been aware of it. This helped bring the extended family even closer together.
- Acceptance of their mom's perception of reality. For example, Georgie had a brief moment of conscious engagement and claimed to have seen friends and relatives who were already dead. Her kids never disputed her experience and reassured her that those loved ones were there to help her. (I have learned that these visions of dead loved ones are not unusual among patients nearing the end.)

By the time I departed, my sense of time and place had disappeared. I felt as if I had somehow managed to melt into the family and the moment.

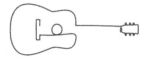

THE FEELING OF BEING CONNECTED with a family never came naturally to me, growing up as I did with almost no bond with my own family of origin, such as cousins, aunts, and uncles, the exception being my two brothers. During the early months of my relationship with Cynthia, my progress in therapy felt slow. Every time I thought I was making a breakthrough a new emotional crisis or obstacle would arise.

One weekend, Cynthia had asked me to drive with her to meet her mom, dad, and siblings at their farm, a three-hours' drive southwest of Kansas City. She had one younger sister and three younger brothers.

It was late afternoon and most chores had been done by the time we arrived. After getting a tour of the farm that included checking on the cattle, we headed back to the house and took our places at the kitchen table. Seeing them all yelling, arguing, laughing, and teasing, I felt totally out of place, never having had that experience in my own family. I couldn't even remember ever gathering around the kitchen table except to eat meals in silence.

Her family was like the TV family on *The Waltons:* expressing loud love. I didn't know how to interact and felt like an alien. I simply wasn't confident within a family setting. The experience left me feeling unworthy. I would soon realize that it was not just intimacy with a woman that scared me, but something much wider.

It was family intimacy.

Family, for better or worse, is the foundation of what we become psychologically. Somehow relationships and family are connected in a way I didn't understand because I had not come to terms with my childhood, having few memories of myself as a kid. For me, family was not a safe haven but a thing to be avoided.

During the drive back from the farm, Cynthia sensed my discomfort and intuitively saw some of the connections that would take me years to fully grasp. She simply said she loved me, which is what she said every time we were together.

The following week, I was at my weekly therapy session when my defenses kicked in. I unloaded about Cynthia's "phony all-American family—straight out of a Norman Rockwell painting."

And then there was her annoying habit of telling me that she loved me all the time. It made me uncomfortable, her unnecessary need to regularly reaffirm our relationship. I asked my shrink, "What's wrong with her?"

He then asked, "Have you considered that what's wrong has more to do with you than her?" I had no answer. He then suggested we try something. The first rule was that I had to acknowledge to myself that she was not the cause of my discomfort. Second, no matter how scared I was of being intimate, I could not break dates with her without a legitimate reason. I had to force myself into intimate situations. Third, I would report all our interactions back to him. He would then talk me through it all.

With his encouragement, I planned a weekend with Cynthia at the Elms Hotel and Spa, an old, elegant, local destination mostly frequented by couples. We both needed a getaway. It would be fun, I thought. However, my old pattern emerged. The closer to the weekend we got, the more nervous I became, thinking I should end our relationship for good.

I knew there was something deeply wrong with me. I recognized that the closer she and I became, the more I wanted to escape. I knew this wasn't rational. Looking back, it's amazing that my behavior didn't cause Cynthia to break up with me instead of the other way around.

About three days before our spa weekend, I was headed home from a client appointment when I drove past a beautiful, old Catholic Church—Our Lady of Perpetual Help. I had driven past it many times, never giving it a thought. This would be the third or fourth time a church would mysteriously draw me in. The first time this occurred had been about ten years earlier, during college. Too much time had passed since then, however, and I was simply too unaware to recognize how this had happened before.

I parked my car and walked through the front door and entered an empty sanctuary. Sitting in a pew in the middle of the room, I scanned the many stained-glass images along the walls, assuming these were biblical scenes from the New Testament, a book I had never read. I later learned that these scenes which are found in most Catholic churches are called the Stations of the Cross. The next thing that caught my eye was a giant cross with a life-sized carved image of the body of Jesus. Seeing the figure's bruised, bloodied body dangling high up in the air, head drooping down in either pain, exhaustion, or death was a powerfully frightening image. Yet, I couldn't stop staring at it, peacefully transfixed. I spent about half an hour in the church, gradually soothing my anxiety. Soon after leaving, I changed my mind about canceling the weekend with Cynthia.

Cynthia has told me that our weekend at the Elms was when she knew we would be married. The first night we had taken a long walk on the hotel grounds. Stopping, we laughed, teased, held hands, and then it happened: I had a childhood flashback, a new memory. It was of myself, probably under four years old, standing by the front door inside my family's apartment in the Bronx in New York City.

In this memory, I am waiting for my dad to come home from work. The door opens and in he walks, tall, muscular, and wearing a business suit. Excited to see me, he bends over to lift me up as I jump into his arms and we embrace one another.

This memory popped into my head in such vivid detail, as if it had always been with me. And at that moment with Cynthia on the walking trail, a feeling of love and safety overcame me. There was no fear or anticipation of disappointment.

This would be the first of a handful of recollections that would surface that weekend.

19 Harold Gives Me a Warning

WALTER DONALDSON AND GUS KAHN, "MAKIN' WHOOPEE," 1928,
PERFORMED BY EDDIE CANTOR

Name: Harold
Age: Unknown
Diagnosis: Slight dementia

Harold grew up on a dairy farm in Lincoln, Illinois, in the 1920s and 1930s. He played football at Kansas State University. When I entered his room, he was wearing a sweater and a ball cap, each bearing the KSU Wildcat logo. I asked him about this, and he explained that he was a Kansas State University Wildcat football player, as if he were playing in the current season. Also, he let me know that eleven days before he was married, he had five teeth knocked out of his mouth at a game.

I teasingly asked, "When was this, 1910? Didn't you have a face mask?"

He said it was 1941 and, "No . . . no face masks back then." He was immensely proud of having had all those teeth knocked out.

Shortly after this exchange, I walked to my car to get a guitar amplifier because the nursing home wing in which his room was located was too noisy. Upon my return, Harold mumbled something about my going out there to make love in the car's back seat. Kind of surprised, I asked him if I heard that correctly. He said, "Yes, making whoopee. . . . Can you play the song?" He explained to me that the song is a warning to men about the trap of marriage and family responsibilities. He wanted me to know what I was getting myself into if that's what I was doing in the car.

Harold was quite a character. I visited him three times over the next few weeks. His two daughters and their husbands were also with us at times, singing along with the music. The entire room dynamic changed with them singing, talking, and laughing. It really brightened the sessions for Harold. On my fourth visit, he turned me away. He simply wasn't in the mood for music and was on his way to join some buddies in the facility's activity room. That was the last time I saw Harold.

The city cemetery is located close to Harold's nursing home. I drove past it when visiting him, each time thinking it was strange to have placed hospice patients so close to a cemetery. Who wants to be reminded when death is so close? Eventually, I realized it might be comforting for some to know that others have traveled this path. I tried to embrace this for myself as well, accepting that I too am on this journey.

During my first year as a beside performer, prior to knowing Harold, I was in a comfortable state of avoidance about the prospect of my own mortality, even though my hospice clients were an ongoing reminder. It wasn't until my sessions with him that I also began to realize I would never truly get into a client's space and walk the road with them unless I confronted my own fear and uncertainty about death. Music may have opened a door between me and my clients but walking through it to meet them forced me to look at my old demons. Part of that challenge was looking through the windows of my past. That history has often been framed by my relationship with music.

As Cynthia and I grew closer, my guitar playing took new turns. Tiring of all the old rock songs I'd been playing for years I began exploring original fingerstyle arrangements in unusual tunings on my acoustic guitar. These are commonly known as *open tunings* and do not rely on traditional standard chord configurations, giving the music a different sound texture.

At the time we were bonding, a burgeoning genre of music was emerging that I liked: new age music. There was no exact definition of this music. With some exceptions, the songs in this genre do not often adhere to repetitive melodies or "song hooks" like most pop hits do. This form of music can be very ethereal, and its aim is to establish a sound texture that evokes a certain mood within the listener. It was also described as *ambient sound.* It seemed to enhance meditation and relaxation techniques, also providing an environment conducive to alternative spiritual practices, energy work, massage, and yoga. Mostly instrumental rather than vocal, the traditional acoustic instruments that seem to lend themselves to this style are guitar, piano, harp, violin, and Native American instruments like flutes, drums, rasps, and bells. Certain eastern instruments are also widely used, such as sitar, tabla, and tamboura.

A few folks still call this musical style new age. The genre is also known by various other names, such as transcendent music, earth music, celestial music, and even spa music. The style as it has evolved, never became one that most people listened to all the time, but rather at certain times and places when and where inner calmness is their objective.

It makes sense to me today that in order to compose or perform this type of music one must possess a sense of inner peacefulness and be able to channel it through an instrument.

My chaotic emotional life, high-driving, type-A personality, and general need for structure and control made me an unlikely candidate for the expression of such music. Yet, I managed to compose one song in this style. It was such a beautiful piece that I surprised myself. The first time I played it for Cynthia she got teary eyed before asking me to play it over and over again. The song may have been the catalyst for a marriage proposal.

Soon after hearing it, we went to our favorite bar. Surrounded by noisy tables, she said she wanted us to marry. It did not sound like a question, but rather a strong suggestion accompanied by all her reasons. In my typical controlling fashion, I told her I wanted to be the one doing the asking. However, I did counter by asking if we might live together first, as a trial arrangement. That was the unconscious reemergence of an old behavior— strengthen the attachment without a lasting commitment.

Cynthia was wise in saying no. Knowing about my previous relationships that had involved cohabitation, she simply asked, "How did that work out for you in the past?"

A few months later, I popped the question, thinking it would be a joyful surprise. With no romantic setting or preproposal speech about how much I loved her, I simply said, "Will you marry me?" After patiently waiting weeks for me to get my act together, her response was, "So . . . is that it? Is that all? Is there more?" Then she said yes.

As for the song I had composed months earlier, I soon forgot how I had tuned the guitar to get the right sound texture. I also forgot the notes and still don't recall the song's name. The composition literally evaporated from my mind. God must have removed it after it served its purpose.

My proposal was accepted on a Sunday morning. That afternoon, we drove to Cynthia's family's farm to share the news with her parents. The main purpose of the visit was to ask her father for his blessing. Being the type of person who rarely asks anyone's permission to do anything, in my mind that was a relinquishment of control, a sign of weakness. I made sure Cynthia understood that I was not asking her dad for her hand in marriage or his permission. This would be more of a courtesy call, an acknowledgment of his very traditional viewpoint about most aspects of life. I told her I was "basically just letting him know."

She rolled her eyes at my phony confidence and said nothing.

Devout Catholics, her parents had just returned from church when we pulled onto the gravel road leading to the house. I had purchased a bottle of Canadian Windsor, her dad's favorite brand of whiskey, and nervously took it with me to the barn, where I found him doing his Sunday chores. He was cleaning up the building and shoveling manure. I walked in, bottle in hand, and said, "Hello, Marvin." He didn't say hi back to me. Nor did he try exchanging any other pleasantries. That was never his style.

Marvin nodded to acknowledge my presence and just stared at the bottle in my hand and me. I told him it was a gift. "A bit early for that, don't ya think?" he replied. I stuttered a bit and let him know why I was there. "Marvin, Cynthia and I want to get married. We just wanted you and her mom to know." Calm and reserved, he said nothing, figuring I had more to say.

After an uncomfortable pause, I asked, "How do you feel about that?" His response was direct and blunt. "How am I supposed to feel about my daughter bringing home a New York Jew?"

Yikes! I thought, not knowing how to respond.

Then, with a backhanded compliment, he quickly followed up, saying, "Well, you're probably the best thing she's dragged home." With no smile, he looked at the bottle still in my hand and said, "You need that more than I do." With that, he turned around and resumed shoveling shit.

20 The Man Who Knew Over One Hundred Interesting Celebrities (One Way or Another)

Virtually every writer I know would rather be a musician.

—KURT VONNEGUT

Name: Frank
Age: 87
Diagnosis: Parkinson's disease and senile degeneration of the brain

As a bedside musician, I learned early on to be flexible and not take everything that a hospice client says too seriously, especially if they have some type of degenerative brain disease. Although suffering with any type of life-ending illness has its indignities, it helps to have a sense of humor. At the same time, it is not wise to discount everything said by a client no matter how farfetched. Some have lived fascinating lives worthy of a book.

When I first entered his room, Frank was lounging on his bed watching the NFL Playoffs: New England vs. Kansas City. He was glued to the TV and I could barely get his attention to start a conversation. With eyes on the screen, he repeatedly told me how much he loved football and especially the Kansas City Chiefs. I couldn't bring myself to let him know that the game he was watching was a repeat. It had already aired four days earlier and the Chiefs had lost.

I turned on the TV's channel guide and saw that he was watching the NFL Network, which would air that same game multiple times—right up until Super Bowl Sunday where the Chiefs would not be appearing.

That's the way it is with folks suffering from various types of dementia. They can't recall events of the prior few days even though they might recall life events of fifty years earlier. Frank probably watched that same game when it first aired the prior Sunday and had no memory of it. Thus, every time he watched, it was fresh and exciting for him. Just like the movie *Fifty First Dates*, where a man falls in love with an amnesiac and has to win her love afresh every day.

My guess was that he would probably watch it over and over until they stopped airing it. And by the time he watched the Super Bowl, he would have forgotten the outcome from all the playoff repeats he had already seen.

We watched the remainder of the game together and I played songs during the commercial breaks.

Frank was born in the small farming community of Council Grove, Kansas, in the 1920s. He told me about his younger days playing clarinet and saxophone as a working musician in a dance band during the '40s and '50s. Also, that he had been the sports director at a radio station in Wichita, had attended the West Point Military Academy, and had worked at a Kansas City advertising agency. The most amusing parts of his tales were when he'd casually throw in the names of all the famous people—actors, musicians, comedians, and TV and movie stars—he'd met throughout his life. He said there were hundreds more who were friends and acquaintances.

Months after our visit, I got curious about Frank. Searching online, I found his obituary. He had died just a few weeks earlier. Most of his achievements were true. He had attended West Point and was, in fact, a radio sportscaster and a musician whose band entertained troops during World War II. His ad agency was part of one of the largest in the world, with him rising to become its president.

Sometimes I find myself searching the names of clients online, to see if any of the more suspect tales they tell me about themselves might be true and verifiable. While searching Frank, I found myself on Amazon where I found a book authored by him still in print that describes his relationships with over a hundred celebrities.

For whatever reason, few of my clients have had careers in what I would call creative business services, like advertising, graphic design, TV, radio, publicity, marketing, entertainment, and promotions. When I visit with those who have these kinds of backgrounds, I'm reminded that having an aptitude in any of these areas can bleed over into an individual's personal life. That was certainly the case while Cynthia and I planned our wedding and exchanged wedding vows in front of about 150 people.

The wedding represented how creative one must be in making concessions to family and facing financial challenges. My mother seemed pleased that Cynthia and I would be married. Although the ability to emotionally bond is severely stunted in people with schizophrenia, Cynthia was the one person, other than my brothers and I, with whom she could express at least a limited degree of affection. However, she made it clear that, as a Jew, she would not attend a wedding in a church, or one presided over by a Christian pastor or priest.

I had pretty much stopped caring what my mother thought years earlier, and just did whatever I pleased. If she didn't attend my wedding it would be one less person to accommodate. It would also eliminate the possibility of a disruptive and embarrassing outburst on her part during the event. Cynthia, however, had a different attitude on the matter. She had a friend whose husband was a judge and also happened to be Jewish. He agreed to officiate what would essentially be a secular ceremony. There was no reference to specific Christian or Jewish themes.

The ceremony and reception would be held at a local racquetball club because their event space was nice and also inexpensive. My father, mother, brothers, and work colleagues attended. Of course, we seated my mom and dad at opposite sides of the hall. Cynthia had about forty family members in attendance, mostly from South Dakota. Most of the remaining guests were movers and shakers in the local advertising community. Many were actually my competitors who worked at area radio and TV stations. Each had relationships with Cynthia since she was an important client to all of us. Many insisted on attending the wedding so they could honor her with gifts. Cynthia understood why this was so important to them and we happily sent them invitations.

One opportunistic radio station came up with the "Cynthia Litwer Honeymoon Incentive Plan." If Cynthia spent enough advertising dollars with them, they'd give her an all-expense paid honeymoon package to Hawaii. Since we lacked enough money for both food and liquor at the reception, a honeymoon getaway would have been out of the question if we had to pay for it ourselves. I encouraged this scheme of mutual exploitation.

Along the same lines, both of us being in the advertising industry, Cynthia and I hatched the idea of trading corporate sponsorships to our wedding in order to save money. This would entail including two sponsors in the invitation copy and a prime position in a wedding handout. In return, they would provide products or services that we would otherwise have to pay for. One of my radio station advertisers was a beer distributor who agreed to provide beverages at the event. The only other client I could interest was a funeral home. They agreed to provide limousine transportation for the wedding party and anyone too drunk to drive home.

Both these sponsors had a sense of humor, seeing this as an unusual publicity scheme. However, common sense and dignity won the day, and we did not follow through with our plan. We would find the money to pay for these things elsewhere.

The wedding was something of a cultural mashup: a sea of cowboy hats and string ties interspersed with black tie and designer suits. A local nightclub pianist friend provided traditional soft music for the ceremony. Immediately after was a surprise appearance by a local marching drum corps, performing highly choreographed dancing and acrobatics to the songs of Michael Jackson. This was followed by a well-known local radio personality acting as disc jockey, playing country music and rock and roll for the remainder of the evening.

Cynthia's dad sold a steer to help us pay for much of the wedding. But we still didn't have enough money for everything, so we eliminated the food. By the end of the evening people were puking from drinking too much on an empty stomach. Too drunk to walk, our limo driver had to assist us from his car into our home. A week later we were on the beach in Maui.

Our original wedding invitation, which we did not use, read as follows...

The Honor of Your Presence Is Requested
at the Marriage of

Steve Litwer and Cynthia Aasby

~~~~~~~~

Proudly Presented by:

Bocksteiner Beer of Kansas City
&
Horowitz & Sons Funeral Home

21 Sleepy Gene's Old-time Gospel Hour

Music is a higher revelation than all wisdom and philosophy.

—Bettina von Arnim

Name: Gene
Age: 87
Diagnosis: Heart disease and dementia

Before I play, I try to pray. My typical preperformance prayers are usually brief appeals for an easy patient interaction, the ability to be present and be smart about the music I choose, and for my performance to be error free—simple requests. Soon after I began this practice, I recognized that these prayers were mostly focused on me and what I envisioned I needed for a fruitful musical visit. On the day I first met Gene, I therefore finished my prayer with the phrase *according to your will.*

I had been contemplating the similarity of the Christian and Hindu notions of surrendering one's expectations to a higher force. This way of thinking seems to acknowledge God's ultimate guiding hand in all things and a sincere desire to let go of one's own desire, submitting in all ways to His mysterious plans. Thus, I gave the new language a whirl.

I had been told that Gene was a Navy veteran who liked to sit in his wheelchair and doze off. When I arrived, the activities director at the facility told me that his musical taste ran toward old country music and gospel hymns.

Gene was not in his room when I showed up. I found him sitting alone in his wheelchair in a large TV-viewing room with lots of couches, stuffed armchairs, and nice art on the walls. The TV was muted, and the room was empty. In these types of situations, I almost always ask someone to move the client to his own room so we can have undisturbed quiet time and avoid interruptions by staff or other patients. I don't like having to field requests for different types of music from many people all at once. Thus, the decision to stay with him in the TV room was out of character for me.

Gene didn't have much to say, so, after a brief introduction, I played some of the mellow songs I thought we'd both enjoy. I completely ignored his preference for country and gospel music. It wasn't in my plan. He immediately fell asleep. A few minutes later, he opened his eyes and without a word, rolled himself out of the room, leaving me seated alone there with the guitar. Patients do this type of thing sometimes. They get bored or distracted by whatever is going on in their mind.

I figured, *What the heck,* so I kept playing for myself, knowing an orderly would eventually bring him back. Sure enough, Gene was caught wandering around the hallways and rolled back into the room where he quickly fell asleep again.

Thinking it might liven things up a bit, I put down the guitar, set up my portable speaker, and opened up a music app on my phone. First up was a collection of country gospel hymns by Alan Jackson. This sequence woke Gene quickly. However, the volume also attracted others, something I had not anticipated. One by one, other patients, hearing the music from surrounding rooms, wandered in, some using walkers and others, wheelchairs.

I ended up with an audience of about twelve people. Feet were tapping and hands were moving about in the air for an hour of gospel hits. Three women, Carol, Pat, and Beverly, were singing, clapping hands, and applauding after each song. One even shimmied to the music. Half the audience was swaying and singing off key to any given song. Then some staff joined us, one with a tambourine.

I soon realized that Gene had once again disappeared, but I was too involved to go find him.

One unexpected patient interaction took place on a couch in the corner of the room. I keenly watched a woman being approached by a gentleman who appeared to be trying to snuggle with her. She responded warmly by grabbing his wrist and pulling him in. A staff person quickly came over and the male lovebird quickly jumped off the couch like a teenager who had been caught violating the rules. I have come to learn that unexpected relationships take place all the time between patients in healthcare facilities, some very intimate.

As I departed, I discovered Gene sleeping peacefully in his chair in the next room. During my drive home, I talked with God about His changing my plan, from being an isolated guitar player for one sleepy patient to a digital DJ at an old-time revival meeting. Nothing about this visit had unfolded as I wished or expected.

The spiritual forces that act upon our human existence are mysterious but very real, whether they be from God or the Universe, however one chooses to frame the source. The simple expressions *Thy will be done* and *According to your will* are, I believe, both a powerful submission and an invitation to these spiritual forces. It makes it easier to give up one's preconceptions of outcomes and allowing these forces to work through and around you.

One of my early discoveries about Cynthia when we were dating was her deep involvement with astrology, the study of the movements and relative positions of celestial bodies. These are interpreted as either having an influence on or reflecting human affairs and the natural world. When meeting people, she'd sometimes ask about the date of their birth in order to better understand them. If they showed an interest in learning more about themselves, she'd also get the exact time of birth and location for an in-depth consultation. I was surprised at how many people displayed an interest.

I initially took Cynthia's interpretations of my own personal chart with a grain of salt, figuring it was an area of minor interest, something she studied as a hobby rather than a serious pursuit. To me it was like visiting a fortuneteller, psychic, or tarot card reader at a fair; you might do it for fun. I was disabused of that notion over time as I found her to be overly engaged in studying the personal astrological charts of friends, family, and work colleagues.

Cynthia frequently consulted my chart and her own side by side to understand what might be in store for each of us individually and as a couple. She told me this type of analysis identifies the life lessons we each had to learn and highlights our behaviors. She explained that a chart reveals the blueprint of the energy operating in our lives, and certain opportunities for change and growth.

She claimed that when approached from a psychological perspective, astrology is a tool for understanding human behaviors. For example, my Sagittarius Sun in the tenth house indicated leadership roles in business and a career-driven life. My Mars, Moon, and Venus are in Aquarius in my chart, reflecting not only my experiences with my mother, but also my detachment in relationships. Aquarius is the sign which describes, basically, all that is different from the status quo, or "normal reality." There were also spiritual aspects of a life that a chart could reveal. Her explaining my chart to me led to discussions of her belief that we are all vibrations living in tune with the universe, affecting and being affected by what we cannot see, but with purpose. "We are all spirit, matter, and energy in an orchestrated dance created to love," she would say.

After we were married, our conversations approached the metaphysical dimensions of astrology and I began to quiz Cynthia about why and how this system worked. She'd simply say, "I don't know, it just does." Once I asked if astrology's determinism might be in conflict with Christian views on free will. The predictive nature of astrological interpretation seemed to me to challenge the idea of a God with a plan for each of us. "Nonsense," she said. "Astrology and Christianity are both parts of God's bigger plan and, therefore, there can be no conflict. Fate and free will work in concert with one another."

Cynthia suggested with conviction that the magi in Matthew's gospel were astrologers.

On several occasions, I suggested that seemingly accurate interpretations of an individual's behaviors and life might be nothing more than assumptions by a highly intuitive astrologer. Based upon personal information gleaned through conversations prior to a chart reading, the astrologer would only appear to have special insights based on the person's chart.

Cynthia would quickly dismiss that possibility. Years earlier, she had dropped out of a master's program in psychological counseling, believing that astrology was a faster and more accurate tool for understanding people. She had been just six credits short of receiving her degree.

Cynthia also had an interest in other unconventional practices, such as tarot card reading, psychic reading, channeling of spirits, and the technique of past-life regression, which is a guided meditation that takes one into the recall of a past life. These practices, she said, were simply different ways to approach reality. It wasn't long before I had begun noticing that much of what Cynthia perceived in daily life was filtered through a metaphysical lens—a lens informing her thinking, feelings, conversations, actions, and relationship with God. I understood little of what she would talk about and was bothered that a highly educated, intelligent person would embrace the view that there is a connection between what went on in the skies at the time of our births and our present selves. Also, her suggestion that our personal inclinations could be divined through other practices.

Of course, Cynthia would regularly discuss my personal chart with me. That only heightened my growing discomfort. In analyzing my personality and emotional patterns, I felt she was invading my space. I would often become defensive and angry.

Eventually, a very scary question came into my head. Was it possible that I had chosen my mother in another format— maybe not a woman who was "crazy" in a clinical sense, but a crazy woman, nevertheless? With images of my incoherent mother swimming around, I began to lose respect for Cynthia and became embarrassed as her professional identity slowly shifted from being an advertising executive to an astrologer and spiritual seeker.

Had I just not seen the trouble earlier? She seemed too mystical, unscientific, and superstitious. In today's terms, she was *woo-woo*.

22 David and the Two Cooks

When the night has come
And the land is dark
And the moon is the only light we'll see
No, I won't be afraid, no I won't be afraid
Just as long as you stand, stand by me

So darlin', darlin', stand by me, oh stand by me
Oh, stand by me, stand by me

If the sky that we look upon
Should tumble and fall
Or the mountains should crumble to the sea
I won't cry, I won't cry, no I won't shed a tear
Just as long as you stand, stand by me

—JERRY LEIBER, MIKE STOLLER, AND BEN E. KING,
"STAND BY ME," 1961

Name: David
Age: 62
Diagnosis: End-stage renal failure

My visit to David was the only musical visit I've made that turned into a party. David, a single amputee, having lost part of his right leg, was in his wheelchair waiting for me as he sipped a Coke. We joked about it being filled with bourbon. (He wished!) He was pretty upbeat. He smiled a lot and rocked his head as I played. (He was even tapping his stump that had been resting on his wheelchair seat!) He also hummed along to some of the songs, even though he didn't know them well. Then, unexpectedly, the facility's cook came in the room.

I think she was walking by and just heard the guitar and let herself in. She was totally enamored with the music and sang or hummed along with "Stand by Me." She had tears in her eyes because this was the song that she and her father liked. Tears flowing, she said it was "our song."

Shortly after, another cook came into the room, took my guitar from me, and started playing some bad blues. David loved this spontaneous activity.

Soon before I left, his sister and brother-in-law also arrived, and they got to hear a couple of tunes and we all had a nice chat. They asked me to come back as I was walking out. David seemed really upbeat and talkative throughout.

In my mind, this is the way a bedside music program should work—in a perfect world!

Because of David's relatively young age, sixty-two, he was all about classic pop and various shades of rock music. I visited with him two more times.

On my third visit, he sent me away before I started. He was clearly agitated over something. David died a few weeks later.

Part of the joy of playing for clients is the pleasure it brings to those who may be spending time with them when I arrive. I don't always know in advance if I will be joined by friends, family, or a facility employee. It perks me up having them there, requesting songs they know the client may like when they cannot communicate this themselves.

Beyond that, my performances are also a moment of pleasure or escape for these visitors. It's a break in the many hours of sadness and stress, and sometimes boredom, while enduring the oncoming death of a loved one.

As Cynthia and I navigated the twists and turns of our young marriage, changes were taking place at the radio stations where I worked. I had a great job with no direct reports, which meant I had no hiring, firing, or personnel issues. I was responsible for managing our largest revenue stream, the accounts of big national companies like GM, Ford, and Coca-Cola. This required frequent business travel to New York, Chicago, San Francisco, and Los Angeles to call on advertising agencies. The money was the most I had ever earned. Between Cynthia and me, we had a life of relative abundance.

It all changed quickly when a new upper management team walked through the doors. They were inexperienced leaders straight out of elite business schools. Sent to Kansas City, they were eager to apply their newly earned skills and teach us midwestern rubes. With little real-life organizational experience, their arrogance was matched by their limited people skills. Competent colleagues who had not quickly gotten on board with them were quickly terminated. Others began resigning, including my boss and mentor. I was the last mid-level manager standing.

The new leadership team thought I was smart. They also discovered I was well liked by the remaining employees. Thinking they'd reverse a growing morale problem by doing so, I was offered a promotion that would have me supervising a couple of dozen people. If I accepted the new position, I would be required to sign a noncompete agreement. This meant that if

I ever resigned or if they fired me for any reason, I could not work in the radio industry someplace else for a year.

In most cases, a company that asks an employee to sign such a document will claim that it protects them from an employee joining a competitor and sharing insider knowledge of their practices. In reality though, it's often a power play to make the employee who signs too afraid to accept another job, out of fear of being sued. Thus, they'd be more subservient to the existing employer.

I saw this document as a demand for loyalty. It pissed me off and triggered my old penchant for disrespect and defiance in the face of authority. I made a counteroffer by adding a ridiculous clause to the agreement they had given me although I knew it would anger them. My clause stated that if they fired me for any reason, then they could not hire my replacement for the same length of time I had to remain out of work. I carefully explained the fairness of this: If things did not work out between us, then they would be legally required to suffer for the same amount of time I was required to do so.

They got pissed and immediately tore up the noncompete agreement in front of me, telling me to keep my current position. They also lowered my compensation.

I didn't have to wait long before an exciting new job opportunity would present itself. This was for the position of vice president, the highest level at most radio stations. I met the owners who had been given my name by an ex-colleague. The interview went better than I could have hoped for. They seemed like honorable folks who genuinely cared about their employees. Their station had been very stable and profitable for many years. I knew, having competed against them. The owners wasted no time in telling me that I seemed perfectly qualified and shared that I was one of their top candidates. They made a hugely positive first impression on me and I was eager to move forward.

The next step would be a phone call—not a job offer or second interview. It would be a one-hour call from a screener at a firm that conducts personality testing for companies. My prospective new employer let me know the call would be coming that Saturday.

The purpose of this type of call is to better understand a candidate's strengths and weaknesses from a behavioral point of view, gauging their compatibility with the company. When the call came, there were very few questions about my background. It was mainly an hour of personality questions.

"Are you more introverted or extroverted?"

"Do you hold your friends to certain moral standards?"

"What do you think most people you've worked with would say is your greatest weakness?"

"What has been the greatest disappointment in your life?"

The phone screener asked me to say the first things that came to mind. He also requested that I give short answers. I actually thought this would be a fun way to solidify my standing with my next employer, believing I already knew what they wanted to hear about me.

Cynthia was in the kitchen listening to my answers when she heard me raise my voice and say, "None of your FUCKING business! What does that question have to do with anything?" The screener ended the personality assessment call almost immediately.

Cynthia knew what had happened. She came into the room and calmly said, "He asked you about your relationship with your mother, didn't he?" My response had been a kneejerk outburst. It was as if someone had quickly punctured an unhealed wound and out poured venom.

A few days later, I received a call from the radio station owner. He very politely told me, "Steve, I can't have someone like you overseeing our people." I told him I didn't know what he was talking about.

23 Grace Notes

The music is not in the notes, but in the silence between.

—Wolfgang Amadeus Mozart

Name: Dorothy
Age: 93
Diagnosis: End-stage COPD

When I knocked on Dorothy's door and announced myself, instead of a customary greeting like, "Come on in," or "Are you the musician?" what I received was, "You're two minutes late!" After my apology, she simply smiled, and we exchanged some small talk. I often tell folks up front that I have never been a professional musician; that I'm basically a self-taught guitarist and an unpaid volunteer. That's my way of lowering their expectations. Dorothy challenged that notion when she said, "Don't worry, I won't tell anyone about your mistakes." I thanked her for her sensitivity and grabbed my guitar from its case.

The first song in our session was "Spanish Harlem." I asked if she recalled the song and where she was in the early 1960s when it was popular. It's always gratifying for me to discover how many folks in their later years can recall what they were doing much earlier in their lives. They love sharing parts of their personal story. Dorothy told me that she couldn't recall 1960. She was busy raising six children in St. Louis. She then paused and added, "And a husband too." I asked where her kids were today. Meaning, where did they live? She said, "Four are in the area and all are very successful . . . not a single one in jail!"

After playing the song "Las Cruces," I shared that an Australian friend, while touring the United States some years earlier, composed it while performing in Las Cruces, New Mexico. Dorothy quickly told me that the song title means "the crosses" in Spanish. She also said that as you enter the city of Las Cruces from the east, there are large wooden crosses on the southeast corner. She had spent a lot of time there while on family vacations.

For our remaining time, I played very soft songs. Songs like "The Water is Wide," "Sleep Walk," and a medley of three Beatles songs: "If I Fell," "In My Life, "and "I Will." I finished with "Shake Sugaree," a lullaby by the folk-blues guitarist Elizabeth Cotton.

Dorothy asked about each song and laughed aloud at her own funny comments. That alone kept me smiling. It's rare for me to visit a dying person, especially one very near the end of their journey, who displays such a hearty sense of humor.

Before I departed, she told me that she was listening for my grace notes. It's a musical term defined as an extra note added to a melody for embellishment or ornamentation. I found this interesting because she had told me earlier that she had never been a musician.

I played for Dorothy one more time before she passed.

What I remember most distinctly about my time with Dorothy was her comment about grace notes. For some reason I kept reflecting on the term until it occurred to me that just as in music, our lives have grace notes. Perhaps they are the nuances of our personalities that repeat themselves throughout our lifetimes and that end up giving us our own distinct flavor as people. Or maybe they're the special gifts we possess that become our own special embellishments to what might otherwise be seen as ordinary lives.

Perhaps a grace note is a pattern of circumstances we are drawn into. I am still searching my past, as far back as I can, in order to recognize my own grace notes.

Cynthia never gave up trying to convince me that astrology might offer valuable insights into my personality. She would share aspects of my life gleaned from my chart, like how I'd always be financially secure. I tried to politely listen but was usually too doubtful to ask about the entire concept of astrology to make any genuine effort to understand. I stubbornly refused to take her seriously. That aside, she already knew too much about me to be objective.

Finally, out of frustration with my resistance, she asked if I would visit with another astrologer, someone who knew absolutely nothing about me. That person was Gina Zelchek, a long-practicing Kansas City-based astrologer purportedly with very advanced skills. I agreed, seeing this as a way to test the validity of astrology by comparing the chart interpretations of both of them. I trusted Cynthia not to divulge any personal information, nothing about my health, family, friends, and hobbies, where I grew up, or what I did for a living.

On a November day, Gina and I met at her home. We sat at her kitchen table and she studied my chart as we briefly chatted. I was especially careful not to tell her anything of substance about myself as this would force her to interpret my chart with no external input. Would her gleanings of the meaning of my chart be similar to Cynthia's? Would they be personal and accurate? I made sure to take notes.

Many of Gina's interpretations in such areas as how I handle money, relationships, and my odd mix of introverted and extroverted behavior were similar to what I had heard from Cynthia. However, Gina expressed them in broad generalizations that made me doubt the accuracy of her reading. For example, it was one thing to say, "You'll always earn a good living." But couldn't that also be true of many people?

There were a couple of things she said that were surprisingly specific and accurate on a personal level. She not only knew I had difficulty in family relationships, but targeted my mother, observing there might be some type of disorder that ran in my family.

I quickly became suspicious that Cynthia had shared more with Gina than she should have. If not, how did Gina have these details about me? The probability of guessing correctly about my mother was low. About 5 percent of the population suffers from a serious form of mental illness. Thus, if Gina was simply taking a wild shot, then she had a 95 percent chance of being wrong. But she wasn't. My session was nearly over when she said she had one more thing to share, "You'll be leaving Kansas City on or around March sixth next year."

When I got home, Cynthia wanted to know how it went. We discussed everything and I shared my notes.

A few months after my chart reading, I received a call from the president of a company that owned radio stations in cities all over the country. He said my name had been passed to him as a possible candidate for an anticipated job opening. After multiple interviews, he offered me the position, asking if I could start on March 9. It didn't take long to decide. I would need to leave for Memphis, Tennessee, on March 6.

24 The Woman Who Knew Things

The Mississippi Delta
Was shining like a national guitar
I am following the river
Down the highway
Through the cradle of the Civil War . . .

I'm going to Graceland
For reasons I cannot explain
There's some part of me wants to see Graceland
And I may be obliged to defend
Every love, every ending
Or maybe there's no obligations now
Maybe I've a reason to believe
We all will be received
In Graceland

—Paul Simon, "Going to Graceland," 1986

Name: Janette
Age: 83
Diagnosis: Congestive heart failure

When assigned a patient, I often have little information about them. I'm always told their age, gender, and diagnosis. Beyond that, there might only be a few brief facts, like whether they are married or have children or grandchildren living in the area. On occasion, I'm told their religion, if that is important to them. For obvious reasons, their taste in music is always a huge plus when the hospice folks can find that out. I rarely receive information about any unusual skills or interests. Janette was raised in Oberlin, a small Kansas farming community near the Colorado and Nebraska borders. That's all I knew about her.

She met me at her front door when I arrived. As I entered, she cheerfully welcomed me with, "Hi, Steven!" She said it loudly with such exuberance that it surprised me because she was such a petite, thin, and frail-looking person. Pulling a room-length oxygen tube from behind her and across the floor, she led me through her living room. On our way, we passed a stairwell leading to her basement. Janette quickly swerved away from it. When I asked why she did this, she simply said it had spooked her the entire time they lived in the house. I asked how long that was and she said, "Two years." Before moving in, they had lived in a trailer park for twenty-nine years. Perhaps having lived in a trailer for so long, she was unaccustomed to basements.

As I scoped out the living room for a suitable playing space, I made a point of telling her that the only person who had ever called me Steven the way she greeted me at the door was my mother. To everyone else, I was just Steve. She paused a moment, and said, "Yes, sort of like Tommy instead of Thomas, or Bill instead of William. But it is much better to use the full and official version of one's name. Your mother knew that much even though she maybe couldn't know other things." I was pondering the strangeness of her response when her husband walked through the room on his way out to leave for his job as a school bus driver.

Ted stopped to introduce himself and let me know that his Janette liked all types of music, although he personally was a western music fan. He said I would have fun playing music for her. I had not yet removed my guitar from its case when he asked about the model. I told him it was a Martin CEO-4R that I had bought about fifteen years earlier. He then shared that his brother had a 1940's Gibson J-45, a valuable instrument.

Janette spoke up and insisted that my guitar probably looked a lot like that old Gibson. It took a few days of reflection to realize that my Martin guitar was a limited-edition model with a body shape designed to look exactly like a vintage Gibson J-45. At Janette's home, I had not yet taken the Martin out of its case when she compared the two guitars.

Extrasensory perception or ESP is often called the sixth sense. People who claim to have ESP almost always describe it as the receiving of information not gained through the ordinary physical senses. They simply know things. Usually included in this category of phenomena are telepathy, uncanny intuition, or supernormal awareness of objects or events not apparent to others. Janette possibly had superior ESP.

After a little small talk, I played the song "Spanish Harlem." Janette knew the song immediately. I was about to tell her it was a song by Ben E. King, but before I began my sentence she said, "I suppose your next song will be "Stand by Me," also by Ben E. King?" That was precisely what I had decided to play next.

There are millions of recorded songs. What were the odds? Even if she knew who Ben E. King was, and wanted something else by him, she could have guessed any number of his hits, including "There Goes My Baby," "Save the Last Dance for Me," and "This Magic Moment."

We continued with the music and, between songs, talked about our families. When it was time for me to leave, she thanked me and said, "I'll see you next week." I knew that was unlikely because I rarely see a patient a second time. When I do, it's usually weeks or months into the future. However, the following week, my hospice volunteer coordinator told me that she might arrange another visit with Janette in a few days.

During my second visit with her, we spent more time talking than sharing music. After a few songs, I put my guitar down and asked if she believed in coincidences. "Not really," she said. "As Albert Einstein said, 'Coincidences are just God's way of remaining anonymous.'"

Here is what I recall of the rest of our conversation that day.

Me: "During our last visit, how did you know I was going to play 'Stand by Me'? And how did you know that I would return without having already arranged it?"

Janette: "I'm psychic. I've always had this ability to know things were coming."

Me: "Can you share some examples of other events in the future that you could see?"

Her: "It's not usually that cut and dried. I often just sense very small, usually insignificant things."

Me: "Are you a religious person?"

Her: "Yes, was raised very Catholic."

Me: "Is there a conflict with being a Christian and believing you have psychic abilities?"

Her: "Why would there be a conflict?" (She looked at me as if it was a stupid question.) "I also believe in astrology and other things."

After this brief exchange, we discussed our favorite music. I told her that I loved all types of guitar music. She asked me to play some Chet Atkins and Les Paul. When I told her their music was way beyond my ability, she suggested some simple old-fashioned acoustic blues, the kind of stuff (she said) that Muddy Waters and other bluesmen were playing in Memphis and throughout the Mississippi Delta and hill country, before much of that music moved to Chicago and became electric. I asked her how she knew about all this and she simply responded, "I read a lot."

Growing up White in rural Kansas, Janette was probably raised on a musical diet of country music. She told me she had never left the state, so it was curious that she referenced an early twentieth-century, regional style of Black music for which I had a particular fondness. Memphis is where I experienced my first meaningful professional success. But during my years there, I did more than hone my career skills. It was there that I became educated about important things that would alter my life: among them, how to live as a racially aware person in a largely racially insensitive world. I had landed in a place where I learned about the artists and entrepreneurs who helped to melt the racial divide by creating a revolution in popular music.

In Memphis, Blacks comprise over 50 percent of the entire metropolitan population and 65 percent of the population of the city itself. As a point of comparison, Blacks comprise around 13 percent of the entire U.S. population. Memphis crossed the minority-majority threshold years ago.

Upon my arrival, these demographic numbers were mere statistics to me, significant only from a professional standpoint. I had moved there to lead advertising sales at two radio stations, both of them programmed for Black audiences and I had to have a grasp of these kinds of numbers to share with potential advertisers. These two radio stations commanded the largest number of listeners in the market. How tough would it be to sell advertisers such a large audience of Black listeners in a community that was predominantly Black? I would be one of the handful of White employees out of around fifty.

One of the two radio stations I worked for was WDIA. This was where I discovered how little I knew about the evolution of Black music and its eventual impact American popular music. In 1948, WDIA became the first radio station in America to be programmed exclusively for a Black audience. It was a revolutionary idea at the time. Prior to that, Black Americans had no way to hear the music that most appealed to them except at live performances or on records specifically marketed to them. Songs by Black artists originally targeting the Black audience might occasionally find their way onto a local radio station, but for the most part, the music was thought to be unappealing to mainstream White audiences. The recording and broadcast industries had labeled it *race music.*

Race music was broadly made up of blues, jazz, and gospel music. At WDIA, proud of its historic legacy, I learned that White and Black artists had actually been covering one another's songs and successfully repackaging them for years prior to WDIA. In 1948, the year the station launched, the music industry replaced the term *race music* with *rhythm and blues* (R&B). With R&B, gospel, and large doses of Black-oriented news and public affairs programming, WDIA quickly became the most listened to radio station in Memphis and throughout the Mid-South. This was primarily because it initially had no competition for the attention of the region's massive Black population.

Some of WDIA's early disc jockeys were also musicians who would become nationally known. These included B.B. King and Rufus Thomas. Not bound by old, racially based programming practices, the station even aired White artists whose styles were compatible with Black tastes. Unlike many White listeners, fewer Blacks were put off by music by White artists. WDIA claimed to have been the second radio station in America to play an Elvis Presley record: his first hit, "That's All Right Mama." Recorded in 1954 at Sun Records in Memphis, it was originally written and performed by fellow Mississippian and Black blues artist Arthur "Big Boy" Crudup in 1946. With that song, Elvis fulfilled Memphis Sun Records founder Sam Philip's long-stated dream: "If I could find a White man who had the Negro sound and the Negro feel, I could make a billion dollars."[1]

When I arrived in the 1980s, WDIA was still a legend among the hundreds of other Black-targeted radio stations across the country that it had once inspired. It had evolved into a programming mix of urban oldies, gospel oldies, and news/talk appealing to an older audience. There were also around five other Black-formatted radio stations in Memphis. Just as mainstream radio had splintered into different listening formats, so had Black radio, with each station programmed to appeal to diverse tastes within the Black community. After years of living in the lily-White Midwest, my music and management education had newly begun. At the same time, my three-year-old marriage was coming undone.

The stress of a cross-country move and the self-imposed pressure of achieving greatness in order to avoid professional failure strained my relationship with Cynthia. While she was calmly adjusting to our relocation, on a daily basis I was bringing home my work-related anxieties, which triggered my defensive coping mechanisms. I virtually laid my stresses on her shoulders, projecting my issues on her, wanting to know why she wasn't as diligent at building an income as I had become. Evenings became screaming matches as I began to wear her out.

The more strained things became at home, the harder I worked at my job. My extreme fear of failure turned into unrestrained ambition. Success came quickly and within a couple of years, I received a great deal of industry recognition as the radio stations' revenues soared. Yet, it seemed that my failure at home was inversely proportionate to my accomplishments at work.

Just three blocks from my office on Union Avenue in Downtown Memphis, I experienced the revival of one of America's most fabled music districts, Beale Street. In the 1920s, Beale had become the urban cradle for blues. By the late 1940s, Chicago had lured away many of its most gifted musicians; and by the 1960s, Beale would fall victim to the urban blight that claimed so many of America's native music districts. It eventually devolved into empty bars and shuttered storefronts. In the late 1980s and 1990s, a full-blown revival was in high gear. With its architecturally restored buildings, restaurants, theaters, and blues clubs sprouted up. For me however, it was the street music that gave the area its flavor.

Every major city has them, but a reinvigorated Beale Street now had an unusual concentration of street musicians—you could see them block after block in all directions, playing day and night. They mostly played blues on inexpensive acoustic guitars, helping to revive the district's unique authentic character. I'd stroll up and down Beale at least once a week, buying cheap lunches from street vendors, stopping often to listen to music. Unlike many guitar players, most Beale Street musicians did not use plastic picks to pluck the strings, just the fingernails and flesh of their right hands.

Like most of the early Delta blues masters, the thumb on the right hand would play bass notes while the remaining fingers played chords and the melody. This is a difficult technique to master. With just the right hand, it attempts to replicate the fullness of a piano, which allows the player to use all ten fingers of both hands simultaneously to play bass lines, melodies, and chords. This authentic playing style came to be known as *country blues,* a subgenre of American roots music.

A few years later, Eric Clapton would expose modern audiences to country blues with his *Unplugged* album.

If WDIA was the grandfather of Black radio in America, keeping classic Black programming alive, then WHRK, its FM sister station, was the hyperenergetic contemporary grandchild. When I walked through the doors, it was WHRK that had been introducing the Mid-South to a newer musical form exploding across the racial divide: hip-hop. Ice T, Grandmaster Flash, T La Rock, LL Cool J, Kurtis Blow, the Fat Boys, Run DMC, Salt-N-Pepa, the Geto Boys, Public Enemy, and N.W.A. were among the newest generation of Black music's superstars. At that time, WHRK had the largest share of listeners of any Black station in America. And, just as blues, rock and roll, and soul had crossed over and done so much to extinguish musical racial distinctions, a large portion of these artists' fans were young Whites.

Hip-hop, too, had crossed the color line.

My exposure to all this music became a history lesson. The evolution of blues, soul, and rock and roll that took place in Memphis had made it one of contemporary American music's great legacy cities. I once counted the number of songs that reference its name. There are over a hundred. Among them:

- "Memphis, Tennessee," Chuck Berry
- "Memphis Beat," Jerry Lee Lewis
- "Back to Memphis," Chuck Berry
- "That's How I Got to Memphis," Tom T. Hall
- "The Memphis Train," Rufus Thomas
- "Graceland," Paul Simon
- "Big River," Johnny Cash
- "Hotel Lorraine," Otis Span
- "Memphis in the Meantime," John Hiatt

- "Memphis Soul Stew," King Curtis
- "Beale Street Blues," W.C Handy/L. Armstrong
- "Carl Perkins' Cadillac," Drive-By Truckers
- "All the Way from Memphis," Mott the Hoople
- "Furry Sings the Blues," Joni Mitchell
- "Talk Memphis," Jesse Winchester
- "Honky Tonk Women," The Rolling Stones
- "Going Back to Memphis," The Memphis Jug Band
- "Johnny Bye-Bye," Bruce Springsteen
- "Blue Yodel #9," Jimmie Rogers
- "Dixie Chicken," Little Feat
- "From Galway to Graceland," Richard Thompson
- "Memphis Yodel," Jimmie Rogers
- "Memphis in June," Hoagy Carmichael/Nina Simone
- "Memphis Blues," Louis Armstrong
- "I'm Going to Memphis," Johnny Cash
- "Music Makin' Mama from Memphis," Hank Snow
- "Night Train to Memphis," Roy Acuff
- "Stuck Inside of Mobile with the Memphis Blues Again," Bob Dylan
- "Big Train (from Memphis)," John Fogerty
- "Walking in Memphis," Marc Cohn
- "I've Been to Memphis," Lyle Lovett
- "North Memphis Blues," Memphis Minnie
- "Memphis Monday Morning," Bobby Blue Bland
- "Proud Mary," Creedence Clearwater Revival
- "Whisky Rock-a-Roller," Lynyrd Skynyrd
- "Memphis Streets," Neil Diamond

How Cleveland became home to the Rock and Roll Hall of Fame instead of Memphis is a mystery to me.

25 All Blues Ain't Blue

I'm goin' to Kansas City, Kansas City here I come
I'm goin' to Kansas City, Kansas City here I come
They got some crazy little women there and
I'm gonna get me one

I'm gonna be standing on the corner,
of Twelfth Street and Vine
I'm gonna be standing on the corner,
of Twelfth Street and Vine
With my Kansas City baby,
and a bottle of Kansas City wine

—JERRY LEIBER AND MIKE STOLLER, "KANSAS CITY," 1952

Name: Rachel and Suzie
Age: Mid-80s
Diagnosis: Alzheimer's disease

Some types of dementia can decrease inhibitions and the ability to control impulses. I had read about this but rarely have observed that type of behavior during my bedside visits. The literature on this states that a patient's decrease in inhibitions sometimes creates aggressive or unkind, blunt, rude, or even vulgar behavior. I also learned that, on rare occasions, a patient may actually become more outgoing, friendly, or unusually affectionate.

When I arrived at Sunny House Assisted Living, Rachel was in her wheelchair in a TV-viewing common area with other patients, mostly women. Most were engaged in different ways, some watching TV, some chatting with each other, some talking to themselves and a few simply napping in recliners. Rachel didn't want to leave her friends for a private bedside performance in her room, so I was asked by the home's activities director, if I might perform for everyone in the common room. I didn't know the background of anyone except for my client. Certainly not all were terminally ill. When the activities director turned off the television and introduced me, Rachel rolled up her wheelchair a few feet, directly in front of where I had seated myself. She wanted a good view. Some smiled and mostly just stared at me, waiting for something to happen. Others paid no attention.

I'm never certain what to play in these situations, with a group of folks each with different conditions. This type of audience adds an entirely new dimension to the challenge of "reading the room." However, my client seemed cheerful, hungry for some music and I decided play something out of the ordinary for me.

I started with "Kansas City," the 1959 hit blues song recorded by many artists, like Fats Domino and Little Richard, and even the Beatles. Rachel and some of the other female patients loved it. Some tapped their feet and clapped their hands to the beat. Rachel even stood up from her wheelchair and did a slow dance, unsteadily shuffling around me. To my surprise, she leaned into me and started kissing me on the back of my neck. Slightly uncomfortable, I gently moved away, and she went back to her wheelchair. I then changed my song list to a more mellow selection.

A few months later, I was visiting eighty-three-year-old Suzie at another care facility. I was told by her hospice social worker that she rarely interacts with people, almost never communicating verbally. Suzie displayed very little engagement with me during our session, mostly sitting quietly in a chair in her room. Eventually, I grew bored playing my typical repertoire of soft acoustic melodies and decided to liven things up, figuring it would make little difference to her mood. I played the driving and very familiar blues classic (and Chicago Cubs Wrigley stadium favorite!) "Sweet Home Chicago."

Oh, baby, don't you want to go
Oh, baby, don't you want to go
Back to the land of California, to my sweet home Chicago

Now one and one is two, two and two is four
I'm heavy loaded baby, I'm booked I gotta go
Cryin', baby, honey, don't you want to go
Back to the land of California, to my sweet home Chicago

—ROBERT JOHNSON, "SWEET HOME CHICAGO," 1937

At the end of the song, Suzie surprised me by getting out of her chair. Quickly shedding her red sweater, which she threw my way, she shouted, "I'll go! I'll go! Baby, please take me to that land of milk and honey!"

As I think about Rachel and Suzie, I wonder if these two particular songs challenge some assumptions about the music people will likely enjoy if they are of a certain age and with a condition like Alzheimer's disease. Even my own notions have been challenged. Playing just about anything appropriately matched to a patient's mood even if unfamiliar, may spark a physical response or conversation. The blues as it turns out is one such style that can have a positive impact on a patient. The other thought is that the themes of both of these blues songs are virtually identical. Leaving, moving to another part of the country for opportunity, getting a fresh start and reinventing oneself. It's the great American migration story set to the blues. Did these remove some condition-related inhibitions? Not all blues is "blue."

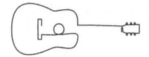

LONG BEFORE MOVING TO MEMPHIS, Cynthia and I discussed what she might be thinking in terms of her own career. She had recently quit her advertising job before the Memphis opportunity had appeared. She said she hadn't given conventional jobs much thought. Like most couples, we relied on two incomes. My increased pay from the new job actually was close to what we had earned together, but I felt she needed to work as well. When I eventually pressed her on this, her answer was brief, "If I just want to sit around talking with spirits, that's what I'll do." I thought she was either teasing or testing me. Either way, that answer didn't reassure me. Her response told me she would resist any pressure to get a regular paying job on a timetable.

After a pause, she also mentioned actively developing an astrology practice. I understood that if she chose to do this, at least she'd stay busy pursuing something she loved until finding something conventional; maybe even make some money doing personal chart readings.

Today I realize that this move was never viewed by Cynthia as a chance to rebuild a conventional career with her advertising skills. That was never her vision. Our move to Memphis held the promise of a different long-held dream. But I was too narrowminded at the time to see this. All I could think of at the time was how her unorthodox interests might affect our financial security and my own status. I figured she would eventually come to her senses.

Within the year after our move, Cynthia did get a job. She became a camp counselor at the Memphis Jewish Community Center. She worked shepherding five-year-old boys through their morning summer camp. She also began to teach classes in astrology and attracted some clients who paid her to read their astrological charts and got referrals from many of them. A local metaphysical store contracted with her to write a monthly column on astrology. Much of her remaining time was spent engaged in an all-out metaphysical exploration—a quest to discover herself and connect with God, which was her true lifelong ambition. For this pursuit, she studied Hinduism and eastern mysticism and began dabbling in various esoteric divination systems, from exploring the power of crystals and psychic phenomena, to channeling spirits and reading tarot cards.

While reaching out to local astrologers, Cynthia met an assortment of other metaphysical types: healers and seers. Even without knowing these individuals, I could identify them on sight, wearing clothes with celestial images or with a certain earthy, hippie feel, sometimes displaying tons of bangles or jewelry made with crystals or astrological symbols. A Native American dreamcatcher hanging from a car rearview mirror was a dead giveaway. To many mainstream folks, metaphysically oriented people appeared both weird and lost in their personal search for enlightenment. I don't know that there was a definitive term for these seekers. Today they are sometimes referred to as *woo woos*. I was doubtful about all of them. I couldn't explain to anyone who asked, why these practices were worthwhile because I wasn't convinced myself.

Back then, and still today, alternative beliefs and methods for spiritual growth were considered antithetical to conservative Christianity. However, these folks have never been a single homogeneous group with a codified set of beliefs. Many identify as Christians and reconcile traditional Christian viewpoints with whatever other practices they pursue. In their view, for example, just as the field of psychology is not inconsistent with Christianity, neither is astrology or meditation. Each is merely a tool for self-understanding or enlightenment. For these eclectic seekers, it's about pursuing what feels right to you and the freedom to change your spiritual beliefs or practices if something else makes more sense.

The years Cynthia and I lived in Memphis would turn out to be the most difficult period of our marriage, filled with misunderstandings heaped upon more misunderstandings. It's where all my defensive, self-protective mechanisms from childhood flipped into high gear. At the end of each workday, I'd come home eager to share what was going on with my job. Because she had a background in media and advertising, Cynthia easily related to my challenges and successes. I, however, could not reciprocate. My eyes would glaze over when she'd discuss her soul-searching discoveries. Also, I was disinterested in some of the likeminded friends she was collecting. They had interests and belief systems that were incomprehensible to me.

One day I came home from work and found her randomly tossing stones in our home, trying to divine their meaning from the way they scattered. I nearly lost it, feeling that she had checked out of reality. Not long after, she informed me that she had been discovering how the great eastern mystics throughout history practiced sexual abstinence in order to help purify themselves and attain self-realization. In hindsight, I might have jokingly suggested an alternative practice; why not engage in even more sex as a spiritual practice to enhance the sacredness of our marriage? However, I was in no joking mood.

Unable to recognize her deep desire to connect with God, I experienced her idea as a personal rejection. I angrily suggested that if I had wanted to be celibate, I would have become a Catholic priest and at least gotten paid for my sacrifice.

Looking back, I've come to realize that it was merely a discussion she wanted us to have and not a decision. She had been reading how monks, priests, and other seekers try to abstain from sex and was curious about it. I didn't care about any of that. My defensive filters blocked any good that might have come out of that chat. Feeling that she was punishing me for my disinterest in her otherworldly pursuits, I instinctively lashed back, wounding her and increasing our emotional distance.

As with my mother, revenge was my go-to response. I started faking what little interest I had in her personal activities and would often overreact with derision when our discussions veered into metaphysical territory. There was little casual conversation between us, less playfulness, and, of course, no physical intimacy. Any unusual behavior on her part would set me off and my rage presented almost insurmountable emotional challenges to our marriage. I felt betrayed, "stuck with" a spouse whom I mistakenly thought was crazy, rather than the thoughtful loving wife that she had been. Feeling increasingly diminished and disrespected by my frequent angry outbursts, Cynthia at last realized that the consequences of marrying the child of a mentally ill mother were far greater than she had ever imagined.

For Cynthia, the lasting solution to life's struggles can only be found at a spiritual level. Though it would take me years to understand this concept, she understood it back then and believed that a way to tame our emotional turmoil might be identifying a conventional religious path we could share. Through Cynthia's brief job as a camp counselor, we had met and become fast friends with a few Jewish folks soon after moving to Memphis. Cynthia thought that joining them at Friday night temple services might do us some good. Although raised devoutly Catholic, she encouraged me to explore my Jewish roots and said she would participate.

It had been years since I had been to a temple service, so I felt little connection with the Jewish faith and culture. Having grown up in a dysfunctional secular household, cut off from my extended Jewish family, I had never bonded with other Jews, often feeling like an outsider when in groups with them. I would never have recognized this on my own, but I longed to be part of a community, so I agreed to give Cynthia's idea a try.

Cynthia embraced Judaism. I joined her in taking basic Judaism classes, and she opened up to it as another of the many spiritual paths she explored. She adapted quickly to the community and created relationships everywhere. The synagogue's rabbi fondly labeled her "The Mystic." For myself, glimmers of childhood connections appeared.

As a kid, I had been bussed to Hebrew school at a synagogue three afternoons a week directly following public school. There, Rabbi Wexler schooled us in Torah and the scriptural stories behind Jewish holidays and rituals. I was also taught to read and write in Hebrew. My religious education ended with my bar mitzvah at age thirteen. This was the same year my parents divorced, the period when prominent symptoms of my mother's mental disorder began to emerge. It was also when relatives began disappearing from our lives.

Although I was religiously educated, there had never been follow up by my parents about my Hebrew studies. There was no attendance at synagogue services, not a prayer ever recited at home, and no one ever welcomed the arrival of the sabbath. Religion seemed meaningless and Jewish studies a time-wasting bore. After my bar mitzvah, I had made the decision to never again set foot in a synagogue.

In Memphis, I found myself once again reading prayers in Hebrew. It had been over twenty years since I had held a Jewish prayer book or bible in my hands, yet I had not completely forgotten the language. I also joined the temple's music group, the Temple Bethel Social Justice Band. Led by the cantor, an ex-hippie, we performed pop songs of love and social justice within a Jewish context. I seemed to be doing the things that many Jews do, but I was not quite there. A feeling of spiritual connection with something transcendent was missing.

26 "Do you believe in miracles?"

Rock of Ages! cleft for me,
Let me hide myself in Thee;
Let the water and the blood,
From Thy riven side which flowed,
Be of sin the double cure,
Cleansing from its guilt and power.

—REVEREND AUGUSTUS TOPLADY, "ROCK OF AGES," 1763

Name: Melinda
Age: 55
Diagnosis: COPD

Most of my musical visits take place at healthcare facilities that are cheerful environments for patients and their families. These are usually neutral in terms of decor in order to have the widest appeal. I like their orderliness.

The feeling is different when you are in someone's private space and surrounded by the things that are most valuable to them. These material things—their furniture, art, books, knickknacks, family photos, and other artifacts—give you a sense of their interests and personal tastes and the life they are leaving behind.

My hospice volunteer-supervisor, Rachel, decided to join me on a visit, something she does every few months to see how I'm getting along and how I interact with clients. Melinda, the dying woman we would be visiting, lived in an old working-class neighborhood with many pre-World War II homes. Lots of old cars and pickup trucks were on the streets and in driveways. Few homes had garages, and many were not well cared for on the outside.

It was a cold December day, just after Christmas. Because of a recent storm, I had to carefully navigate the ice and snow on the stoop leading up to the front door. I am usually pretty upbeat when I am about to visit someone, hoping for a positive interaction. However, on this visit, my usual positive attitude was nowhere to be found. I found both the neighborhood and the house dreary, leaving me to speculate about the people who lived there.

As with many client visits, I had to remind myself to pray.

Praying is not something that comes naturally to me because of how I was raised. Thus, when I remember to pray, I pray that the client be at peace and not in pain, and that I will somehow know what words to say and songs to play, even if the client is unable to engage with me. Basically, I ask for the inspiration to interact in a way that provides my listener some comfort or even joy. Due to forgetfulness, my prayers are infrequent.

On this visit, distracted by my own judgmental thinking about the neighborhood and my imminent encounter, I had only seconds to alter my outlook before entering the home. The prayer I said went something like, "Dear God, help me do some good, and not have the client greet me at the door with a gun." I was only half joking about the gun part. Saying such a speed-prayer was more about my anxiety than the patient.

When I knocked, a cheerful voice yelled, "Come on in, we've been waiting!" Rachel had already arrived, and I found her standing beside Melinda, a woman in her mid-fifties, the youngest client I have ever visited. Melinda was sitting on a couch in the living room and fiddling with the tubes on a nearby oxygen tank.

I nervously introduced myself, "Hi, I'm Steve, your musician. Are you in the mood to hear some soothing guitar?" We then exchanged a little small talk. As we spoke, I looked around the room and saw lots of family pictures. On the bookshelves were old hardcover books, some of which were collections of hymns, and a few autobiographies of country music artists from an earlier era. Most striking, however, were the antique instruments lying around: an old-fashioned parlor guitar, a couple of ukuleles, a mandolin. *Nice art,* I thought.

Rachel had already told me in advance that this was Melinda's mom's home and that her mom was taking care of her. Typically, it's an adult child, most often a woman around Melinda's age, who takes care of a parent who is terminally ill. This situation was a reversal of these typical roles. Melinda's mother, Pearl, who appeared to be around eighty, joined us for the performance.

After I played a few songs, Melinda said, "Play some Eric Clapton. I love Clapton." I told her that this was a tall order, explaining that I'm just an amateur musician. Then I asked, "Which Clapton song?" But she couldn't name one.

Melinda made some other requests. "What about 'Take It Easy' by the Eagles? Or 'Smoke on the Water' by Deep Purple? How about anything by the Police or Steely Dan?" Melinda was truly a child of the 1970s. Before I could respond, she circled back around to Eric Clapton and said her favorite song would always be "Tears from Heaven." I told her I'd give it a try.

Next, Melinda asked her mom to play some guitar and suggested we do a singalong. She boasted that her mom was a great musician, an expert in old-time gospel music. The visit suddenly got quite interesting!

Over the next hour, I did my best to follow along as her mother expertly sang and strummed what must have been some of the greatest hits of old time Christian music, none of which I knew: "Jesus Paid It All," "How Great Thou Art," "It Is Well with My Soul," and "Holy, Holy, Holy." All are gospel music masterpieces, some approaching two centuries of age and still bringing grace to American churches. Melinda made sure we also played "Rock of Ages" and "I'll Fly Away," by far her favorites. I had little familiarity with this style of worship music until that day.

After a brief water break, Pearl brought her daughter a set of spoons. Our next set of music featured me on guitar and her mom, who went and fetched an accordion. Melinda kept the beat with the oversized soupspoons. We played more hymns and gospel songs. Everyone played with real feeling and conviction and I was moved in a way I had never experienced during a visit with a patient and their family.

Three times that afternoon, Melinda looked at me directly and asked, "Do you believe in miracles?"

My visit with Melinda and her mom was so uplifting and unusual, that a couple of months after our visit I called my hospice supervisor to find out if I might play for them again. Rachel had been with me on that visit and we had talked a number of times about the specialness of that occasion. She soon got back to me to let me know that Melinda had discontinued her care a few weeks earlier. I then asked if it might be possible for the hospice to reach out to Melinda or her mom on my behalf. Rachel got back to me quickly, saying they had no idea how to reach them. It all seemed a bit mysterious. I still wonder if Melinda had any particular miracles in mind.

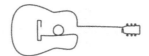

I HAVE ALWAYS BELIEVED IN KARMA, which I once read is sort of like getting what you deserve, as in, "You reap what you sow." Whatever you get, you've earned, good or bad. There's nothing mysterious about that. On a warm May Memphis evening, I also learned about the opposite of karma: grace. Grace is like receiving an unexpected gift that you may not feel you deserve. Within a Christian context, it's the love of God shown to the unlovable.

After the ordinary routines of an ordinary day, I went to bed as always, at approximately 11 PM, leaving Cynthia who was usually an hour behind me at bedtimes. As I drifted off, a clear and familiar voice spoke. "Jesus, reveal yourself." This voice was not merely a thought in my mind; it had the realness of an actual person. Even stranger, it was the sound of my own voice, calling out to a mysterious place. I could hear it speaking but I was not using my vocal cords.

Immediately after hearing myself calling out, instead of the normal blank void that accompanies sleep, with my eyes fully closed, in some sort of liminal state, I found myself staring into a distant white backdrop. It was like gazing directly at the sun if it had taken over the entire sky—an endless, brilliant light.

I was fully alert within my state of sleep, just watching, when a handful of spinning objects appeared in the space between my eyes and the depthless light. The light accentuated their forms. These were geometric shapes, which included cubes, spheres, pyramids, and hexagons, along with other indescribably shaped objects. All these objects were three-dimensional and had rich brilliant colors that I didn't recognize. They were stationary but spinning in space, each a different, glowing color. Some of the colors were beautiful but also unrecognizable.

As I was observing, I became aware that another presence was absorbing everything around me until we were both enveloped in a serene dimension. I somehow knew that Jesus was with me. He was present even though he was faceless and formless. We held each other as I imagine a loving father who knew everything that could be known about his child would embrace him, and me never wanting to let go.

At about midnight, around an hour after I had gone to bed, Cynthia woke me. She asked what I had been dreaming about and told me I had said "Jesus Christ" out loud in my sleep, slowly and with a sense of awe. I just looked at her, startled. She once again asked me what I had been dreaming. I told her about hearing my own voice calling out for Jesus and tried to describe the brilliant white light and unusual colors of the spinning geometric shapes.

She wanted details. But imagine trying to describe the color *red* to a person born blind. There would be no reference point for you to use: the color of a fire engine, a tomato, or blood? None of it would register with someone who had no memory of colors. It was futile describing what I had seen.

"What else?" she asked.

"I was with Jesus," I replied, as if it were as natural as ever.

"Did he speak to you?"

"Yes, we talked."

My wife got excited, wanting to know more, but I couldn't come up with the concrete specifics. It was like describing the colors. There may have been thoughts and words exchanged during my experience, but it felt more like understandings shared by Jesus and myself.

Honestly, I was as surprised by the experience as she was. At the same time, I was enveloped in a state of total serenity. I felt loved.

Cynthia and I stayed up most of that night. I kept trying to find a way to explain that it wasn't the words that mattered between me and Jesus. It was the feeling of peacefulness it gave me, and my deep knowing that Jesus had come to rescue me. Somehow, He and I merged into one another. He was in me and I was in Him.

If Jesus and I had an actual conversation, I didn't remember what was said. Nor did I know where I had been or how long I'd been with Him. I had only been in bed for about an hour, but it felt like an eternity.

That night, I opened up to my wife, perhaps for the first time, sharing previously hidden details of my personal struggles without fear of being exposed as being weak or unlovable. She listened and marveled at the fact that I had had a mystical experience. She was also a bit jealous.

Over the next few days, I was as calm as I had ever been. I had been a heavy daily smoker for years, but now felt no need for cigarettes. The addiction was simply absent. I stopped working ten- to twelve-hour days as the importance of my personal productivity seemed to recede. Up to this point, many of my interactions with employees had been transactional, driven by our work process and the need for the completion of tasks at hand and other metrics of group performance. Suddenly, interactions had become more transformational, with a team orientation and a desire for successful collaboration at center stage. I became less demanding and more attentive to what was going on with colleagues.

These types of changes also took place at home.

27 Fifteen Pieces of Advice for the Living

If you cannot teach me to fly, teach me to sing.

—J.M. BARRIE, PETER PAN

Fifteen clients
Age: 74–90
Diagnosis: Various

Most of the clients I visit are unable to verbally engage with me. Either they have an advanced brain disorder or are so close to death they are virtually inert. But some are able to communicate and even enjoy sharing pieces of their lives. When I visit with these folks, I sometimes ask them for an important piece of advice that might help others.

I have paraphrased some of their most common responses, as well as a few I find amusing.

- **Don't be a complainer.** When you share your troubles with strangers, half will be annoyed because they have their own problems to deal with, they don't care about yours. The other half will be glad it's you and not them. If you must talk, keep it within your own family or with only your closest friends.

- **Don't live in the past or the future.** Reminiscing about a past that we can't bring back or focusing on the future keeps you absent from the present, which is all we have at any given time. Your memories or future longings are distractions, not experiences. Learn to enjoy the *now*.
- **Marry the right person.** You will spend time with this person just about every day of your life, so make this decision wisely. Among other things, your personal happiness and financial future will be shaped by the kind of person they are. Divorce can wreck you emotionally and financially.
- **Take better care of yourself.** Simply taking care of your health can prevent most illnesses. You only have one body, mind, and spirit. When someone else must take care of you due to not taking care of yourself, you pretty much have no freedom left.
- **Learn to cook at least one great meal.** Give it a name. (Mine is Steve's Famous Cream of Smoked Turkey and Wild Rice Soup.) Pass out the recipe. At least you'll be remembered for this one thing.
- **Don't worry so much.** At the end of your life, how you look, what other people think of you, how much money you have, what the future holds won't matter.

This was the most common piece of advice among clients. One told me it is mentioned throughout the Bible and quoted a verse from Matthew (6:25):

> *Therefore, I tell you, do not be anxious about your life, what you will eat or what you will drink, nor about your body, what you will put on. Is not life more than food, and the body more than clothing?*[1]

After a little investigation, I found that variations on the theme of "Do not worry" or "Fear not" appear over 300 times in the Bible.

- **Don't work so hard**. We thrive on love and friendship. No one near the end of life says, "Gee, I should have worked longer hours." Most regrets are about the time they could have spent with their family and friends.

- **Roll with the punches.** Make lots of plans for everything you want to do and then go with the flow and expect nothing.

- **Plan for your own death.** With all the grief and emotional chaos that may surround your passing, one of the most difficult tasks for family members is taking care of funeral arrangements. It's not something most of us do on a regular basis and adds to the stress that already accompanies such loss.

- **Don't miss the chance to talk with your grandparents**. They have seen a lot of things and probably made more mistakes than you and your parents combined. It'll give them a great deal of pleasure. They will only be around for a little while.

- **Don't make decisions when you're angry**. People cheat on their spouses or quit their jobs when they're angry.

- **Focus on the right things.** Don't give much thought to the little annoyances that won't make a difference in the long run. Learn to recognize what "big things" really are— serious illness, financial hardship, loss of friendships. When looked at this way, you will wish you hadn't sweated the small stuff.

- **It's okay to ask for help.** It doesn't make you look weak; it makes you wise.

- **The best time to start is now.** Time gets away from us very quickly, and before you know it many years have passed, and you didn't do those things you wanted to do. Avoid future regrets.
- **Don't neglect your teeth.** It takes time and effort to brush and floss. Better to take the time doing this when you are young than losing them later. Plus, they're expensive to fix!

Collectively, these clients represented over 1,200 years of life experience. Common sense suggests that a wise person consider all the advice they can get. For a good part of my life, I lacked that wisdom. I often took others' advice with a grain of salt. I almost never sought it out. That was one of the residual effects of being raised by a mentally ill person—lack of trust. Deep down, I was often skeptical of the general advice offered by an older person unless they were some type of credentialed expert. That lack of trust only results in unnecessarily going it alone and making a lot of avoidable mistakes. Today, I can use all the advice I can get. It's a treasured gift so many clients have given to me and which I can pass on to others.

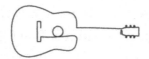

NO ONE KNOWS PRECISELY what causes schizophrenia. No single gene or combination of genes leading to the disorder has ever been identified, but there's little doubt that a genetic component exists because of the disorder's high concordance in families. Within the overall population, about 1 percent is affected by schizophrenia. The number jumps to about 13 percent among first-degree relatives, such as the sick person's children. Among relatives like nieces and nephews the rate is about 4 percent. The rate among grandchildren is about 5 percent. A first cousin of mine was diagnosed with the disorder.

During our time in Memphis, Cynthia and I talked a lot about having children. However, that discussion came with a nagging thought. *What if I am carrying the gene?* As long as I could remember, never far from the surface was the thought that the symptoms might someday emerge in me. Now the concern was for my future children. Telling myself the odds were low, we moved forward anyway, trying to get pregnant, but after a few months, we looked at adoption. For many couples, it is a wrenching decision that affects multiple aspects of their lives—physical, spiritual, emotional. We had no such struggle. We each had thought about it independently many years earlier, even before our marriage. We saw it as a loving way to build a family, regardless of whether we had our own children. The adoption decision was almost a relief for me.

When we visited with a local adoption agency, we were told up-front that the wait for a healthy infant was often two to three years and sometimes longer. We thought that would be too long. We were in our mid-thirties and feeling a sense of urgency. During that conversation, we asked the agency social worker what other options we might have. She quickly responded, asking if we might consider raising a *special needs* child. That is sort of a catchall phrase for kids who are difficult to place for adoption. The term covers children with physical limitations, emotional challenges, and other disorders. It also includes children with a history of neglect and abuse or who were prenatally exposed to drugs or alcohol and with the symptoms that often correspond. Older sibling groups are also in that category, since many folks are not prepared to take two or more older kids into their homes. We asked how many kids fit those descriptions and who takes care of them until homes can be found. We were told that approximately half a million kids at any given time are in foster care or in residential children's homes and institutional settings. Many would never have a permanent family.

After thinking about it, we were not sure we could handle these types of children. Maybe we just didn't have enough love and sacrifice built into us. Feeling somewhat glum about the prospect of being permanently childless, we discovered another type of child that falls into the definition of special needs: biracial. Given the region where we lived, that typically meant a child with one White and one Black parent. It was explained to us that most White couples looking to adopt don't consider any but healthy White infants. These folks often wait years or go out of the country where they might spend tens of thousands of dollars navigating a foreign adoption process. Moreover, there was always a shortage of Black families seeking to adopt. When they came forward, they usually claimed one of the large numbers of available Black kids. Thus, biracial kids often fell through the cracks.

Before making a firm decision, we sought the advice of close friends and professional helpers. I had been seeing a therapist at the time. He gently suggested the odds for a successful outcome in both marriage and parenting for someone like me, the child of a person suffering from schizophrenia, might be somewhat daunting, regardless of any challenges of being a mixed-race family. He also wanted to know if my future children would be interacting with their grandmother. I ignored his observations and the question, refusing to engage in a conversation that seemed designed to discourage us.

Cynthia and I also visited with a second adoption agency to get a second opinion about special needs adoption. That conversation did not last long. The adoption counselor, a social worker, was Black and said she'd never place a biracial child with a White family. She explained that biracial kids were better off in foster care or remaining in an institution, rather than in the home of a White couple where they would never have a sense of their identity as a Black person. She believed they'd grow up confused and alienated from both Black and White communities, and not accepted by either. We could not argue the pitfalls she described. It was the 1980s and social mores in parts of the United States had not advanced for a comfortable acceptance of being biracial or having a multiracial family. It wasn't as ordinary as it is now.

Today over 10 percent of all children identify as biracial, growing up in multiracial families in just about every corner of the country.

The most disappointing response we got to the idea of adopting a biracial child came from the rabbi at our synagogue. I'm not sure what we expected to hear—perhaps some type of encouragement that weaving together a family regardless of the skin color of its members would be a blessing. Instead, he told us that most biracial kids are considered and consider themselves Black. He then enumerated the social difficulties we would encounter as a mixed-race family, offering no spiritual or religious perspective. I responded by suggesting that in a perfect world there would be enough Black families to adopt Black and biracial kids. Embracing his point of view, all you end up with are rejected children and childless families. Thus, the alternative choice should be obvious: Place them with stable, loving White parents who are sensitive to the issues and deal with challenges as they arise. He went silent.

Three months later, our household was blessed with the arrival of Stephanie Claire Litwer, a three-week old infant born to a seventeen-year-old Memphis White girl and her Black boyfriend. She was delivered to our front door by Mindy Roth, the social worker who counseled us from the beginning of our adoption journey. It was March 8 at 7 PM when our doorbell rang, and in she stepped, cradling our baby, who just stared into her new mother's eyes when handed to her. Pure joy in a blanket.

28 The Converts

As you begin to realize that every different type of music, everybody's individual music, has its own rhythm, life, language and heritage, you realize how life changes, and you learn how to be more open and adaptive to what is around us.

—Yo-Yo Ma

Name: Saul
Age: 74
Diagnosis: Pulmonary fibrosis

Saul was one of those clients whose rare lung condition had been diagnosed about three years earlier when he was told he might have three to five years to live, maybe longer. Thus, he had a long time to consider his life and death. When I saw him, he had been on hospice service for a couple of months. It didn't take long to discover that his main preoccupation was contemplation of his faith and relationship with God. Before I had ever played my first song, he engaged with me on a deeply personal level, telling me of the importance of faith.

Saul was a Messianic Jew. Born a Baptist, at some point in his life he chose to practice his faith as a Jew. This did not mean he stopped believing in Christ. Messianic Jews typically have one of two different backgrounds: The first group is composed of people who have been born into the Jewish faith and observe it in traditional Jewish ways, but who have come to believe in the divinity of Jesus. They look to Him for their salvation and for the salvation of the world. They have become "completed Jews," embracing their Jewish identity as opposed to being Christians in any traditional sense. The other group of adherents come primarily from a variety of Christian denominations. They maintain their faith in Jesus but choose to observe Jewish customs and rituals and live by the laws of the Torah. For Messianic Jews, there appear to be no contradiction or inner conflict in this sort of dual identity.

I listened to Saul describe his faith journey with interest but only shared pieces of my own story, having started as a secular, nonpracticing Jew. When I told him the part about my Jewish background and conversion to Christianity, he really perked up. Almost cutting me off, he quickly moved into an evangelism mode. I never did get to the part of my encounter with Jesus thirty years earlier. I'm not sure why I held it back.

Every time I attempted to bring our session back to enjoying some music together, Saul would ask about Jesus. Did I know Him? Did I have a relationship with Him? I said, "Yes," but did not go into the details. To me, that question is like being asked if I've been "saved." I don't like it. Saul, nearing the end of his life put him into an active state of proselytizing. This very Christian calling is not a tradition practiced by Jews. Most Jews I know are, in fact, put off by this custom.

By the end of our time together, Saul was relaxed, feeling he had done his duty with me.

I am not aware of any guidelines or best practices when it comes to discussing matters of faith and religion with clients. I have made a conscious effort not to wander very far into this territory. I figure that's the job of the hospice chaplains. That attitude may reflect my old struggles with straddling the line of feelings between Judaism and Christianity. Years ago, I tried and failed to reconcile them theologically. I had even briefly explored Messianic Judaism but determined that having a foot in both worlds would not work for me. I didn't want to tell Saul I had rejected the path he had chosen.

About six weeks after my Jesus episode, I accepted a job running a radio station in Charlotte, North Carolina. That had always been my dream job. Stephanie was eighteen months old when our family left Memphis. The three of us were off on an exciting adventure.

Although consumed with new job responsibilities, my mind was never far from my supernatural encounter. I spent months contemplating what had actually taken place in my sleep that night in Memphis. It was an undeniably powerful experience; however, I recognized it was completely out of character and immediately began questioning whether I had simply imagined or dreamed it.

Like most Jews, I knew little about Jesus. The very idea that I would call out to Him in my sleep was mysterious because I had never given Christianity a moment of thought before then. I had never read a word of the New Testament and had never allowed myself to be cornered by proselytizing Christians. I had been attending synagogue services and engaging in other ways with the Jewish community. Why would I have such an encounter at this time?

Also, my family history with mental illness began nagging at me. What if my experience with Jesus was nothing more than a hallucination? I was aware of the high incidence of schizophrenia among the children of parents with the disorder and knew that the symptoms in men usually appear by the age of thirty. I was just a few years beyond that. Like my mother, they often hear voices in their head or believe in things that do not exist in the real world. I wondered, *When is a visit by a deceased messiah a spiritual experience, and when is it a symptom of mental illness?*

Cynthia was the only person who knew about my spiritual experience. She saw it as something sacred and encouraged me to explore its meaning. Although raised in a very observant Catholic family, she believes there is essential unity among most high-level faith traditions as revealed in their respective sacred scriptures. Thus, her love for other traditions had not diminished her belief in the divinity of Jesus or the possibility that He might present himself at any time. She had no doubts about my encounter, which she referred to as a mystical experience, one experienced by many individuals. Yet, I was too afraid to share with anyone else what had happened to me, believing I'd be ridiculed. I had not yet developed trusted friends in Charlotte and friends from Memphis who knew about my mother might make a connection between her sickness and my encounter. I needed psychological or spiritual guidance.

Should I find a rabbi at a Charlotte synagogue? No. That seemed too farfetched, going to a rabbi to discuss an encounter with Jesus Christ.

I decided to test the waters by sharing my Jesus episode with an old Kansas City friend, David Zack. He also happened to be Jewish and, like me, very secular. There'd be virtually no chance of him telling anyone with whom I had regular interactions. I flew back to Kansas City for a weekend and shared everything, including my doubts. David listened and asked questions. After some silence, he tried to shame me out of taking this any further.

"Steve, are you fucking crazy?! How could you believe in Jesus Christ?!" he said. "If people actually believed in the ideas that he is purported to have taught, then how come Christians have spent two thousand years hating Jews and blaming them for the world's problems? Why has tormenting Jews been a sport?"

He ended with a zinger. "As a Jew, how could you join them, knowing what they've done?"

I had thought some of the same things myself.

David went on to ask me if I had any relatives killed in Europe during the Holocaust. Most American Jews are descendants of Europeans who immigrated to the United States shortly before or just after World War II. Many had left behind relatives who disappeared during that war. David then asked, "Who do you think murdered them? If you ask a Christian this question, they say 'Nazis' or 'Germans.' It would be just as true to say Christians did it since Germany was a Christian nation."

Soon after returning to Charlotte, I talked myself out of believing in the significance of my Jesus encounter. Another old friend from Kansas City called me shortly after. He was also a friend of David Zack and jokingly said he had heard some gossip about me: "Did you hear about Steve? He thinks he was with Jesus." He shared what he'd heard, and I said, "Yes I had some type of experience," but said nothing more about it. I was embarrassed.

The more I considered it, the more ridiculous it sounded both that I would call out to Jesus and that He would come to me. I decided not to distract myself further and carried on with my life. Soon afterward, my old behaviors resumed. I started smoking again, anxious feelings about my performance at work returned, I became overbearing with people, and tensions rose between Cynthia and myself. The old Steve was back.

29 The Patient Who Helped Me See

When you play music, you're bringing light into the darkness.

—CARLOS SANTANA

Name: Susan
Age: 69
Diagnosis: Dementia

Susan was one of the younger clients I visited. She was waiting for me in her bed when I arrived. Her memory recall issues must have been mild because she said she'd been excited since being told earlier that week that a guitar player was coming to visit. Besides dementia, she also had severely impaired eyesight and could barely make out my form sitting across the room from her. She was functionally blind. The first thing I noticed in her room was a collection of simple unframed watercolor paintings, each taped to the wall next to her bed. Abstract and eye catching, I figured they must have been painted by an exceptionally skilled grandchild.

Often times, the hospice volunteer manager who assigns me clients only provides some basic information about them, like their age and diagnosis. Occasionally, they also find out a client's favorite music style. I only received one bit of useful information about Susan. She had been a cellist with the Chicago Symphony Orchestra. Upon hearing this I became a bit nervous. I had only played one other time for a person that I knew had been a classically trained musician: Judy, the professional pianist with the electric keyboard in her room. Like Susan, Judy had had dementia, but it was very advanced. She'd been too far along with the condition to make any coherent observation about the quality of my playing. Susan on the other hand, was still very lucid. All I could hope for was that she wouldn't catch too many of my mistakes or be bored by my repertoire of simple song arrangements.

Between songs, Susan and I talked a bit about our families, and she asked about my career. However, when I asked about her work life, she simply said, "Oh, I did various things, nothing notable." She never mentioned playing with a symphony.

As I played, Susan just lay in her bed and smiled with the most content look I had ever seen on a patient's face. I asked how she liked the music. All she said was, "Beautiful," and thanked me. I then asked her if it was true that she played professionally with a symphony. Smiling, she said, "Yes," and shared with me how much she loved hearing live music.

She also told me what she thought about my choice to play to audiences consisting of just one person. Susan suggested that it's a gift from God for someone to have a talent that can be spontaneously shared with others. She made an interesting point that giving music away to others never depletes the giver's quantity. She further suggested there are few artistic expressions where the creation can so easily be replicated.

I thought to myself, *Which of the visual arts can be created and delivered immediately upon request? ("Hey Leonardo, do the Mona Lisa!")*

Susan told me that gifting listeners like herself with a performance is a form of grace. I had never thought about my bedside performances like this—as acts of divine grace.

Before I left, I commented on the paintings that I found to be more and more interesting as I gazed at them while performing. I asked who created them. She proudly said, "Me!" I told her how much I liked her work and she asked me which one was my favorite. I tried to describe the one that really caught my eye. It was an 11' x 17' watercolor with small abstract black shapes that looked like black birds with outstretched wings or maybe they were musical notes with flourishes. Whatever they were, some were flying, and others perched on the sides of what looked like cornstalks of different bright colors. The piece was full of brightness and movement. She told me to take it off the wall and show it to her. As I was carefully retrieving it, I asked her how she could possibly have painted with her near blindness but got no response. She then told me to hold it up to her face, a few inches from her eyes. With excitement, she said, "Birds—that's my favorite too! Take it." When I said I couldn't possibly accept it, she let me know that it was only fair as I had received the grace of giving something to her.

Would I allow her the same experience?

Some people exhibit a genuine degree of calmness and peace that can be felt by others. With these folks, there is no noticeable worry or agitation. Whatever concerns they may have, seem to be overshadowed by a positive energy. Susan emanated such composure. During each of the two times we visited, I felt a sense of her calmness claim me. The phenomenon reminds me of a grade-school experiment where two identical tuning forks are placed next to one another. Striking one tuning fork will cause the other to resonate at the same frequency. I'm sure there is an analogy to be made between certain styles of music and the human brain.

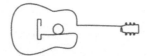

SOON AFTER BEGINNING my new job in Charlotte, I brought Cynthia and Stephanie to the radio station to meet the team, thinking it would be good for them to know my family. A few days later, I was in a meeting with a midlevel manager who had worked there for a number of years. With no context at all, he jokingly referred to Cynthia as Moon Unit. She must have told him about some of her metaphysical interests, like astrology. He might as well have called her a space cadet.

I was embarrassed, not wanting to be seen as an oddball because I was married to one. Regardless, she was *my* oddball!

He thought he was being funny. He was too stupid to realize he had mocked my wife to my face. I quickly found an excuse to terminate him, but not before making him fire most of the team he had assembled prior to my arrival on the scene. I learned early in my career that stupid managers often hire other stupid people. Like attracts like.

These individuals were mostly underperformers with little potential and they were all let go on the same day, so I became known as the Terminator.

I thought those actions would make a bold statement, establishing me as a performance-driven, no-nonsense leader, someone with the courage to upgrade his team when necessary. Instead, my reputation, both among some of the remaining employees and with many of the clients with whom the station had long-term relationships, became that of an insecure and angry manager. Kindness and patience were missing, and I drifted further away from the person I had briefly become during the months following my Jesus encounter in Memphis.

The backdrop to my struggles at work was an ever-present agitation with my mother. I had left her in Kansas City five years earlier, but the passage of time and distance had not altered my emotional responses to her. Now in her fifties, her hallucinations and delusions were milder and less frequent, but the loneliness borne of depression and almost no regular personal contact with others haunted her. She'd call me regularly, begging me to bring her to live with Cynthia, Stephanie, and me in Charlotte. I still reacted to her as I had as a teenager. She was toxic, even over the phone. With each phone call, I'd clam up and become distant.

These calls would last no more than five to ten minutes. My responses were always the same. Initially, I would coldly say, "No, Mom, you can't come live with us." Next, I'd feel guilty about my lack of compassion. Finally, I'd become enraged at her for placing me once again on an emotional roller coaster.

Rationally, I knew her mental illness was not her fault and that she simply needed more companionship. But that logic was not enough to overcome my bitter feelings towards her for what I had endured as a kid. The very idea of living with her was frightening.

The phone calls took place about once a month. After each encounter, I was left edgy and took my feelings out on my wife. During many conversations, I heard criticism, even when there had been none. Any type of intimacy was impossible. Because Cynthia was unable to express her feelings about any of the ordinary annoyances that take place in any marriage without me blowing up at her, she was left more frustrated than ever.

Life at home could not have gotten any worse—until it did. We had been talking about adopting a second child and then

Cynthia realized that it would be too difficult to have two small children to take care of while I was emotionally adrift. With our relationship floundering, she became depressed and her emotional state only made me feel more antagonized.

Having had enough, she suggested I seek professional help. I started by seeing our family doctor who quickly observed that I was clinically depressed and prescribed medication and therapy. Just like my mother so many years earlier, I initially refused.

When Cynthia saw my response, she lost hope in our marriage and told me that she would leave me if I did not immediately follow the doctor's orders. She would not only stop the adoption process we had recently entered, but she would leave me, taking our sweet little three-year-old daughter with her. The ultimatum shook me.

The threat of losing my wife and daughter led me to feel alone, out of control, and abandoned. But I still could not fully comprehend my complicity. It took ongoing individual therapy, group therapy, antidepressant medication, and a deep dive into my family history to begin seeing myself more clearly. At that point, I realized I had no real friendships because, like my mother and father, I didn't reach out to people. Also, I saw that my relationships with my employees were tenuous. There was nothing approaching intimacy in my life with another individual. Furthermore, I had not played my guitar for a couple of years. My interest in music and people had gone flat.

Over a period of months things slightly improved, but not enough. I was still stuck.

One day I asked my psychiatrist if she believed I would ever be able to move beyond my odd hair-trigger defensive mechanisms and abrasiveness with people and overcome my animosity towards my mother. I had been down this road a number of times over the years, but no therapist had taken me far enough. I needed some truth about my prospects for leading a healthy life.

"Have you worked much with folks who have schizophrenia?" I asked.

She said, "Yes, and their children too."

I then asked, "How do the kids turn out as adults?" She was somewhat evasive, telling me that, in her experience, many children raised by a mentally ill parent grow up to be relatively high-functioning adults. I thought this was a vague answer because there are many types of mental illness. I drilled down a bit and then asked specifically about the children raised by a parent with schizophrenia and bipolar disorder.

After a pause, she told me these two disorders are among the worst for patients and their families. When a patient has symptoms of both, they are diagnosed as suffering from *schizoaffective disorder,* an exceedingly rare type of mental illness. It's a mishmash of the worst symptoms of both illnesses. She said that doctors no longer give a separate schizophrenia and bipolar diagnosis, its simply schizoaffective disorder. I had never heard that term before.

She then cautiously explained that the majority of children raised by a person not undergoing treatment do not fare well as adults in any number of ways. "They battle depression and often cannot maintain relationships. Their marriages usually fail, and they typically have unstable work histories. They struggle with most ordinary life issues." In other words, she said, "They are typically *not* high-functioning individuals." When I probed further, she said, "These are often the people sleeping in boxes under bridges."

I told her that her description sounded a lot like my mother, not myself.

She responded by telling me, "The adult children of these folks may not suffer from schizophrenia or bipolar disorder themselves, but as kids they may have learned the sick parent's behaviors in dealing with the world." She went on to explain that many develop self-protective coping mechanisms to distance themselves emotionally from the parent, which are not conducive to healthy future relationships with anyone else. Most take one of two directions. They become very compliant in every aspect of their lives, underachievers avoiding any type of conflict in their lives. Or they take the opposite approach, breaking free of their environment and taking on the world, overly controlling, with a false sense of confidence and an aggressive outward posture. With either type, behaviors are often ingrained so early that they cannot be entirely undone, just managed with the help of medication and therapy.

By this time, I was not liking what I heard. I knew which description fit me. It got worse when she suggested I try taking one of the antipsychotic drugs she uses with her patients diagnosed with schizophrenia to help manage my symptoms of anxiety and depression. It seemed to me like she thought I was a sort of half-baked version of my mother.

I took the prescription the doctor gave me for about four weeks and gained about fifteen pounds in that short period of time. Aside from that, I felt no discernable change in my down mood. I think that's when I first prayed with conviction—maybe out of desperation. Prior to this, I had been too ego-driven and economically successful to surrender myself.

Unfortunately, few people say, "I was so successful I just had to reach out to God." But the mask of false self-confidence I had been wearing all my life had been window dressing.

30 The Sisters of Charity

A man should hear a little music, read a little poetry, and see a fine picture every day of his life, in order that worldly cares may not obliterate the sense of the beautiful that God has implanted in the human soul.

—JOHANN WOLFGANG VON GOETHE

Name: Sister Bernadette
Age: 90
Diagnosis: End-stage renal failure

Among all the individuals and groups for whom I have played, few have touched me like a handful of nuns living at the Sisters of Charity retirement community, a small facility for aging and ill nuns. I visited with the same seven to ten of them four times over a two-month period. With each visit, I got to know more and more about each of them as individuals. That each was struggling with a different condition did not prevent any from coming together to join me for an afternoon of music and conversation on any number of topics. After my first visit, they actually created a Steve Litwer Fan Club, posting colorful handbills all around the facility prior to my next appearance, in order to attract the biggest audience possible, reading: Music with Steve This Thursday!

Initially, I was asked to play just for Sister Bernadette, a terminally ill nun who had lived as a Sister of Charity in Leavenworth, Kansas, for forty-eight years. I was at a loss as to how I would communicate, relate, and interact with her. What would I have in common with an elderly nun so frail and near her end?

I resolved to find out about Sister Bernadette's background from some of the other nuns in the fan club. Born in 1927 in Montana, she entered the Sisters of Charity in 1946. She began her healthcare ministry in Butte, Montana, as a nurse and worked in medical-surgical nursing, obstetrics, infection control, and social services at other hospitals in California, Colorado, Iowa, Kansas, Nebraska, and New Mexico.

When I showed up, Sister Bernadette was sitting in a TV-viewing area with other sisters. The facility's activity director requested that I play for the entire group so they wouldn't have to move her back to her room for a private bedside performance. About seven nuns were present, most not on hospice service, but all with some type of condition requiring care. Most were eager listeners who responded to me in surprising and often amusing ways. Like Sister Bernadette, they had played varied roles during their lives within the Church, mixing religious pursuits with professional pursuits.

One of the women, Sister Agnes, was from Brooklyn, New York. Verbal and sharp-witted, she possessed advanced degrees in physics and mathematics and was outspoken about her views. After I told everyone that I was born in New York City, she recited a quote from a famous New Yorker: "I'm from NY and I know a con man when I meet one." I knew she was quoting ex-mayor Michael Bloomberg, talking about Donald Trump during the 2016 presidential election. She then explained to everyone, "Trump lacks *kenosis*, the ability to empty out one's will to allow in God's love." Sister Agnes' opinions generated discussion among the others who cared about politics.

I never discovered Sister Cecilia's background. She must have had short-term memory issues because every time I visited, she'd ask the price I paid for my guitar and wanted to know if I was willing to sell it and for how much. Sometimes she'd ask these same questions two or three times per visit. She also cried during each song and would applaud afterward.

Sister Louise had a master's degree in music and had directed choral programs for all the Catholic schools in the Archdiocese of Los Angeles for twelve years. Not surprisingly, with few exceptions, she knew the words to most of the songs in my repertoire.

Then there was Sister Anna Marie, who never showed up to our gathering without her laptop. During each of my visits, she was busily typing. I once asked her what she was working on and she responded by letting me know she was scripting her own funeral arrangements. She was planning six separate events and had already written me into one of them to provide some "light entertainment."

At the end of each visit, Sister Anna would grab me before I departed to share the writings of some famous theologian. The German Jesuit priest Karl Rahner must have been one of her favorites because she showed me one of his books in which she had highlighted some passages.

I don't remember the name of the book, but because I liked these passages, Sister Anna wrote two of her favorites on a piece of paper that she handed to me before I left so I could reread them later.

The dead are silent because they live, just as we chatter so loudly to try to make ourselves forget that we are dying. Their silence is really their call to me, the assurance of their immortal love for me.

If we have been given the vocation and grace to die with Christ, then the everyday and banal occurrence that we call human death has been elevated to a place among God's mysteries.

On my final visit to play for the Sisters of Charity, we sang Elvis Presley songs and Sister Louise sang Louis Armstrong's "What a Wonderful World." Sister Anna mused on the nature of music as a personal expression and on the importance of spaces between the notes. And Sister Cecelia cried, again asking about the value of my guitar and if I was willing to sell it to her.

It's usually long after a client visit that I am able to derive some meaning from that encounter. Often it takes weeks or months, at which point I'm able to make a meaningful connection to what was going on or how it meshed with my life in ways I could not see at the time. There was no such lag in time with the Sisters of Charity. I was reminded while there that this was not my first memorable experience with women from that order.

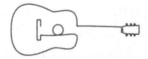

MY DAILY COMMUTE FROM the southeast suburbs to my office in Uptown Charlotte took me north on Providence Road. At about the halfway point, I'd pass St. Gabriel Catholic Church. At the end of a particular day, on my way home, I pulled into the church's parking lot, parked, and entered the building. Unlike a number of past spontaneous and mysterious visits to churches, this time I knew exactly why I was there. I found the church's administrative offices and asked a woman sitting at the reception desk if there was somebody available to speak to me about Jesus Christ. I figured that this would be an ordinary request.

The woman just stared silently at me for a few seconds. Apparently, she was not accustomed to strangers wandering in off the street asking such a question. She looked at me as if I had just asked for a double cheeseburger and fries.

After a pause, the lady asked, "I'm sorry, what's your name and tell me again who you are looking for?"

I left the church a few hours later with a carton containing a twelve-volume set of books on the history of Christianity. When I got home, I surprised Cynthia by recounting details of a spontaneous visit to the church. The puzzled receptionist had eventually fetched a knowledgeable person, an elderly nun named Sister Janet.

Sister Janet had a doctorate degree in ancient Middle Eastern studies and had taught ancient Arabic and Hebrew literature at various universities before retiring. She spent her spare time tutoring students and volunteering at area churches. When she came out of an office to greet me, she wasn't wearing the habit that one might associate with Catholic nuns. Stylish and contemporary, she was dressed like any other professional woman—no long black robe or woman's head cloth drawn in folds about the chin. I told her that I wanted to know more about Jesus and Christianity.

"Why?" she asked.

I shared my mystical experience with Jesus. She then asked me how I knew it was Him.

"I just know," as I described the feelings and experience as best I could.

"What did He look like?" she continued.

"I can't remember His face, just the experience of He and I being a part of one another, somehow united."

"What about your religious background?" she asked.

"I'm currently a nonpracticing Jew. I grew up in a secular family," I said.

She had no comment about that and continued quizzing me, eventually asking what I'd been doing during the days leading up to my encounter. I told her that to the best of my recollection, they were probably uneventful. I'd gone to work as always. After dinner, watched TV before bed. Nothing stood out in my mind.

"Can you recall what you watched on TV?" she asked.

It had been over a year since my experience, but I remembered exactly what I had watched. "It was a weeklong miniseries called *War and Remembrance*," I replied.

She then asked if I knew why I remembered that particular show after all this time. "That's really unusual. What can you recall about the story?" Detective Sister Janet was drilling down, leading me to some answers. It was the one aspect of my evening with Jesus that I had resisted examining until now.

I told her, "The movie takes place during World War Two. One of its story lines was about a Jewish family in Europe, some of whom resisted the Nazis and others who perished. There was a gas chamber scene that was very graphic in the episode that took place the same night as my Jesus encounter. I'm sure I went to bed that night thinking about it—but seeing movies with Holocaust scenes is nothing unusual, as we've all been exposed to that piece of history many times. It may have bothered me a bit, as I suspect it does for most Jewish folks."

"Maybe this time it shook you up more than you want to admit," suggested Sister Janet.

I knew where she was going with this, and before she asked, I told her it would have been totally out of character for me to call out to Jesus for any reason. I believed most Jews rarely, if ever, think about Jesus. Most don't know anything about Him and definitely don't believe He was divine.

Sister Janet gently replied, "But you did anyway, and it sounds like you may have found Him—or maybe He found you? Let me give you some books to read and then you can call me."

After sharing the details of my meeting with Sister Janet, I asked Cynthia if she'd attend the next Sunday service with me at St. Gabriel. Her reaction to all this was one of hopeful surprise. She grew up in a Catholic family but had not been a practicing Catholic since her college years. Regardless, she never gave up her Christian beliefs, even as she explored other faith traditions and metaphysical realms.

Always seeking the hidden meaning of events, she later told me that St. Gabriel was the patron saint of communication—making the connection that I was in the radio business. She also looked at the church's actual street address: 3016 Providence Road. Among Cynthia's many interests was numerology, the belief in the divine or mystical relationship between numbers and coinciding events. The numerological meaning of the number 3016 is "new beginnings" she told me. And finally, she told me, "The very word *providence* speaks for itself."

Six months later, I was baptized into the church. I was fully engaged with my newly adopted faith.

31 "I'm ready and there are those waiting in the wings"

> *A bird doesn't sing because he has an answer,*
> *he sings because he has a song.*
>
> —JOAN WALSH ANGLUND

Name: Caroline
Age: 74
Diagnosis: Liver cancer

Caroline is one of the few clients who had broached the subject of her impending death with me. She spoke about it very easily as someone who had come to terms with it and accepted it as a natural part of life. When I arrived at her room at the care facility, she waved me in and told me to sit down and wait until she was finished with her project. She was propped up in her bed with a yellow legal pad, writing something. I asked her what she was doing, and she said she was picking her meals for the next month. This appeared to be an exciting activity because, as she told me later, "The food at this place is incredible! They don't repeat a meal for four weeks and its gourmet food!" (Food has turned out to be a major topic for many of my clients who reside at assisted living or nursing facilities.)

Caroline was familiar with a lot of recording artists. She had been a schoolteacher who finished out her work life as a tour guide in Branson, Missouri. Over the years, she'd met a lot of the musicians that live in and have visited Branson, performing for the millions of annual tourists. While we spoke, I noticed a huge photomontage of her two sons, their wives, and her grandchildren hanging on one wall. Another wall piece was a giant, oversized Post-It-note from one of her grandkids with a farewell message. I was so moved by this that I could hardly hold back my emotions. We discussed the postcard and her family for about thirty minutes before I even got my guitar out of its case.

Caroline was so upbeat that it lifted my spirits just listening to her share her life story. Then, rather abruptly, she announced that she had to leave for a hair appointment. Many facilities have in-house hair salons as well as libraries, small theaters, art galleries, coffee bars, and lots of other services that give patients and families a feeling of both normalcy and enjoyment. When I started packing up to leave, she invited me to the hair salon to perform for everyone. I accepted and we ended up playing Name That Tune, a fun little game where I'd play the first few bars of a popular song and the patients competed for who could name it first.

When it was time for me to leave, Caroline said, "You're a real charmer. It's good that I only have four weeks left." We said goodbye, but I knew I would want to come back and see her again before she passed.

When I returned three weeks later, she was remarkably calm and lucid as she told me she was "ready and there are those waiting in the wings." She could no longer eat regular solid foods, just light things like Cream of Wheat. She said she was blessed and that there was no pain—just anticipation. She then began to tell more of her life, starting with her name.

Caroline was named after Carole Lombard and Jean Harlow, the hugely famous movie stars of the 1930s. She began college late, at age thirty-nine, at William Jewell College and it took her ten years to graduate and become a teacher. The grandson who did the incredible wall card was just seven years old and she thought she could stick around until she got one from another grandchild.

She said my visit made her day and I told her she made mine too! I then left very calm and with a sense of reverence. Caroline passed a few days after my visit.

I AM OFTEN AMAZED BY THE FACT that I have been married for over three decades. It's astonishing that a person who started out life wounded and with no conception what a healthy family looked like, somehow managed to beat the odds and ended up with a full life and a phenomenal family with (hopefully) well-adjusted kids and grandkids. I had recognized my blessings long before I began playing music for hospice clients, but the cumulative effect of being with these individuals led me to take another look at how I got where I am and what I continue to discover.

It can be a real epiphany when one recognizes how some of life's events, especially ones that were painful or mysterious at the time, are actually unrecognized gifts. Years later they make sense. Significant occurrences do not always seem linear in a rational sense, with cause and effect easily discerned.

I don't think God works that way. Good things often follow other good things for no obvious reason, sort of like running the table in a casino despite low odds. And bad things can come out of nowhere, turning life upside down, just when everything seems to be fine. It can take great distances of time to realize that everything might have had a purpose, none of it random, and none being either good or bad.

Maybe everything that happens is part of a cosmic grand design, although I'm still unsure about that.

Within months of my baptism, Cynthia and I were blessed with the adoption of our second daughter, Ariel Mae Litwer. She was three months old and had been living with a foster family, waiting for a permanent home. The documents that her birth mother provided to the Children's Home Society of North Carolina stated that the family who adopted her should be Christian. I had just converted three months earlier, so we qualified.

Almost a year of therapy and an immersion into Christianity had gone by since Cynthia had threatened to leave me. We began to unify as a family, going to church regularly and even praying at home together. I was as calm as I had ever been and began dealing with my lifelong history of disruptive behavior. Also, the embarrassment that I might be found out as being the product of a mentally ill home was not so strong in me as it once was. However, God was not finished with me.

Just when things began looking bright, there was a tragedy: Cynthia lost her youngest brother to suicide. This loss sent her into a tailspin, and I had no clue about the depth of her grief. With two small children at home and her debilitating grief, she became immobilized, struggling just trying to get through each day. I grew impatient and anxious and even scolded her for not healing from the loss fast enough. I had totally lost my bearings.

The steadiness I thought I was mastering in my newfound faith disappeared. Jesus was nowhere to be found.

I spent weeks wondering why Cynthia couldn't get herself back on an even keel. She went into automatic self-survival mode, with a priority of taking care of our two young children and herself as she mourned. She had nothing left for me. My level of fear and selfishness in reaction to feeling her pull her attention back from me was just one sign of how much further I had to grow. I'm still embarrassed by my inability either to recognize the full extent of her pain or to comfort her during her time of crisis.

Three months later, I lost my job. In a moment of poor judgment, I challenged my boss on what I thought was a wrongheaded management decision. He quickly fired me for being insubordinate. Suddenly, Cynthia did for me what I was unable to do for her. She rallied around me, finding part-time employment writing advertising copy and doing voiceovers for TV and radio commercials to secure income. She wisely knew that coming together as a team was the only thing that made sense. Thus, she cut short her period of mourning her brother's death, for me.

I watched her pray often, a habit I had not yet adopted. I think that's when I really began to pray daily.

It took three months to find a new job. We went back to the city where Cynthia and I had begun our careers, met, and married: Kansas City. We had left almost eight years earlier as a couple. We returned home as a foursome, humbled but hopeful.

32 The Superiority of One Noodle Over a Guitar

> *Music, when soft voices die,*
> *Vibrates in the memory—*
>
> —Percy Bysshe Shelley

Name: Sally
Age: 80
Diagnosis: End-stage cardiac disease

Sally's three adult daughters, Mindy, Chase, and Margarita, were with her when I showed up. While each introduced themselves, I immediately noticed two things: First, the smell of urine. This is not uncommon if an orderly has not been around recently to clean patients who cannot do that for themselves. Scanning the room, I also noticed trophies scattered about, some on a dresser and others on a bookshelf and a bedside table.

After telling them a bit about myself, I addressed Sally to see if she could tell me about herself. She offered no verbal response. She just looked at me and then in the direction of her daughters without turning her head. Nothing but eye movement. They quickly entered the conversation, telling me about their mom.

She had been a social worker, an incredible baker, and a grandmother of five kids, and she loved golf. The primary description was that she had been a competition roller-skating ballroom dancer. I'd never heard of that and found it amusing. They then shared some stories about that, like the time she went to St. Louis with her dance partner and took second place in a regional competition. It was a very big deal.

Throughout the time I played, Sally never said a word. She displayed no facial expressions that might indicate acknowledgment or recognition of the discussion or any of the songs.

That was okay and something I've become accustomed to. My only hope on visits is that the music gets through on some level and brings my listener some contentment.

Near the end of our time together, there was a knock at the door. It was pushed open and in walked Noodle.

Noodle is a pet therapy dog. He was followed in by his owner who had him on a long leash. I knew about therapy animals, usually cats or dogs, being used to assist patients by helping them to relax. I have also watched videos with pet therapy horses being squeezed into patient rooms. Before they can visit patients, dogs must be certified by having gone through special pet therapy programs to teach them to calmly show affection. I have read that animal-assisted therapy can significantly reduce pain, anxiety, depression, and fatigue in people with a range of health problems like cardiovascular disease and dementia, and those undergoing treatment for cancer. These dogs must be very friendly, having a gentle disposition. They often have calming effects on patients.

Noodle, a stunning, red-coated Irish Setter with soft fur, was slowly led to the side of Sally's bed where he sat himself and didn't move. Sally just stared until Noodle slowly lay his head on the bed near her waist and gazed at her with a droopy-eyed look of longing that every dog owner recognizes. Sally looked down and smiled at him. As they looked into one another's eyes, Sally slowly lifted her hand and gently rested it on his head. At that point Noodle sighed, the sound of the dog slowly catching his breath. He seemed to relax alongside her.

I stopped the music and we all sat quietly, enjoying the mystery of their connection.

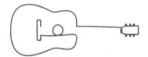

LOOKING BACK OVER A LIFETIME, the years I was gone from Kansas City represent both a death and the beginning of a resurrection. However, I also see those years as a mere slice of the pilgrimage that began as it does for all of us, as a child.

I didn't come to faith easily. There was no early recognition of the signs of a spiritual life to come. Beginning in my college years and beyond, God mysteriously invited me into some of His many homes of worship. I showed up but didn't know why. Later, during my thirties in Memphis, I was called back to Judaism. That was okay for a sense of community but did not turn into a true calling of the heart.

Finally, Jesus entered my life when I wasn't looking. He waited until I was sleeping one night and simply walked through a door and introduced Himself. It was very clever to catch me in such a vulnerable moment. He brought me the gift of grace and a bold invitation to follow Him out into the void so that I could meet God. There was nothing to do other than accept the invitation and later contemplate what that might mean and where it could lead me.

It sounds a bit like having faith. But it was not—not yet. Instead, I repeatedly denied the experience I'd had out of fear of ridicule or worse, insanity. My eventual conversion was a belated RSVP: "Yes, I accept. I surrender. Please take me."

It's been about thirty years since my conversion and I'm still surrendering. During that time, life happened. Back in Kansas City in the embrace of old friends and with a burgeoning career in TV advertising, I experienced something that I had sought all my life—what I imagined to be "normalcy." Because I had not had that growing up, I had no confidence in my assumptions about how average families went about their daily lives and behaved with one another or the meaningful activities in which they engaged. Thus, I did my best to observe and imitate the lives of friends who had qualities I admired, such as humility, honesty, the respectful way they spoke to and about their spouses, and so on. I even developed a new appreciation for family-oriented TV sitcoms, silly as most were, because they gave me ideas on ways to lead an average home life, minus drama.

Thus, I tried lovingly to raise two daughters (plus cats, dogs, hamsters, and tropical fish). I attended their extracurricular activities and practiced being the best husband I could be, took the kids and my wife on annual family vacations, created friendships with our neighbors, and was fully involved in the life of our church. In short, I engaged in all of the day-to-day small and large adventures, events, and responsibilities that are associated with a stereotypical middle-class American life. My only goals were to be normal and average, and not stand out.

On the surface, I seemed to be slowly changing. I was not so impatient, not so quick to lose my temper, not feeling depressed as often. And my career had taken off. I was repeatedly promoted, never having to apply for a single job opening.

Each new position just came to me until I was asked to lead a division of my company. Who would have thought that a guy with so many emotional problems might one day lead hundreds of colleagues? By that time, I was armed with an arsenal of strategies to deal with my old emotional issues: especially insecurity and embarrassment about not being able to explain why I couldn't talk about my childhood years without getting rattled.

I was especially grateful that my mother was no longer living in Kansas City and that my children would not have to spend time with her. My brother, Stu, had brought her to Atlanta, where he had settled. He was married with a stepson and a daughter who had never known their sick grandmother.

Stu was my hero for taking on this responsibility. However, Mom really was only gone in a physical sense. She started to call me, asking me to move her back to Kansas City so she could live with my family. My brother had made a valiant effort to see her once in a while, maybe once every month or two. This was probably as much as he could take of her, and it wasn't enough to alleviate her loneliness and fear of being abandoned.

Each phone call unnerved me just as her calls used to. The sound of her voice on the phone panicked me as it always had. Over the years, with all the therapy I had undergone and taking antianxiety meds, I was still unable to get to the heart of my emotional issues. I just got better at hiding them from myself and others. On the surface, I seemed to be improving, but many of the old memories were still blocked. I could not recall much prior to my twelfth birthday, and my teen years were a bit foggy. I simply accepted that and moved on with my life.

33 A Conversation with My Mother

Music is well said to be the speech of angels.

—THOMAS CARLYLE

Name: Evelyn
Age: 95
Diagnosis: Cerebrovascular accident (stroke)

If someone were trying to get bedside musicians and other hospice volunteers to stop visiting patients, they could not have chosen a better strategy than unleashing the COVID pandemic on the facilities where sick and dying folks often reside. As I was finishing *The Music Between Us,* I had not sat with a client for a very long time. I sensed a lockdown was probably imminent when I visited Evelyn. At the time, I hadn't fully realized the implications for patients and their loved ones, that anything needing to be shared in person would soon be impossible, including a simple "goodbye."

Evelyn was of my last clients before everything changed. She was very calm and seemed to enjoy the music as she drifted in and out of sleep. Stroke victims often experience some pain, but hers was not apparent during our visit. Very few words were exchanged between us, just occasional smiles. With clients who appear to be relaxed and not in any observable discomfort, I find my own state matching theirs, like we're getting on the same wavelength. These are some of my favorite musical visits. I can play softly, matching the tempo of the songs to their mood, and whatever tension I've carried in through the door eventually dissolves.

Around halfway through my time with Evelyn, her daughter Michelle arrived. We spoke softly for a while as her mom dozed. That energized both of us. The daughter, probably around my age, in her sixties, was very affectionate. Speaking to her mom, she held her hand while recounting what great times she had when she was growing up, and how much her mom meant to her. These were very tender moments. While she spoke, I softly played a couple of Beatles songs, hoping they might bring a smile of recognition, forming a sort of historic backdrop to her memories of she and her mom.

I'm easily reminded during musical visits that it's common for a family member to struggle with the oftentimes tedious challenge of spending daily time with a seriously ill loved one. Michelle was grateful for the musical respite (and the Beatles). A few days later, I was informed by the hospice that her mom had passed away.

For a few days after that visit, I thought about my own mom. I imagined us together in a place beyond sadness, pain, and anxiety. There I would apologize to her for my lack of compassion and for blaming her for being sick. In this imagined scene, I tell her nothing was her fault. I tell her I love her, possibly for the first time ever. But I never get a response; she just stares at me with no understanding of what I'm talking about. Still, it's all right. I finally feel forgiven.

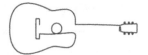

IT TAKES SOME OF US LONGER THAN others to grow into our true selves and recognize what we were meant to be and what to do about it. Some folks are unable to make that leap at all. For some, growth happens in fits and starts.

When I first became a bedside musician, my wife correctly observed that many people feel they cannot do any type of hospice work because they are too uncomfortable being around dying people. Virtually every time she or I tell someone that I am a hospice volunteer, they exclaim how wonderful that is. "How selfless!" they say. I usually respond that there is always a need for hospice volunteers if they are interested. Often the response is the same, "Oh, I could never do that kind of work."

Cynthia has suggested that some of my psychological traits make me perfect for being with dying people. She believes these traits allow me to be unaffected by being with folks whose condition leaves them in some sort of physical or emotional distress, or with those who are too far along to be aware of themselves or their surroundings. The thought of being around dying people is simply too uncomfortable for many potential volunteers.

Cynthia points out that because of my history of having developed a high degree of detachment early in life to protect myself from my mother (and others), I became an ideal candidate to be a hospice volunteer.

In an oddly positive twist of fate or irony, I think there is some truth to my wife's observation. However, I'm also beginning to believe it is not so much detachment as it is *nonattachment*. With the former, one does not fully connect emotionally with others, even as they know intellectually what going on with them. With the latter, you learn to rise above another's struggles as you are connecting with them. You develop an ability to empathize while simultaneously allowing another's pain to move through you.

This is not to say I am always at ease with everyone nearing death. When it comes to the struggles of some, I'm still learning to rise above my own feelings of inadequacy, staying calm and helpful. However, I'm getting better at it. Maybe nonattachment is the superior evolution of detachment. You still feel the others' pain, but it moves through you.

Yet, there may be a stronger dynamic at work, a call to compassion.

It is not just me sharing the gift of my music, time, and companionship. I am also blessed that many patients do me the honor of allowing me to spend time with them as they approach the end of their physical journey. Some delighted to share their stories and know my own. Their time and interest in being with me, too, is a gift of compassion.

And what about the music? The remarkable power of it upon our bodies, psyches, and spirits is still being understood. Are our responses to certain rhythms and sound combinations a product of evolution, or were these with us from the beginning, a creation of intelligent design?

When I am playing, pain and compassion come together. But it doesn't stop there. A kind of circular effect takes place. What goes out to the universe comes back to me in the form of long-buried memories bursting through my diminishing defense mechanisms. These memories, remembered in this grace-filled context, are giving me a new viewpoint about the people and experiences that shaped my life. With my patient interactions informing my memories, I slowly bring a newer version of myself back to future client visits, where I am more at ease, more open, more compassionate, and in every way better able to relate. With each new visit, I have found myself being a bit more vulnerable and humbler.

When people are approached in this manner, they, in turn, feel safe to share their own vulnerability. No amount of therapy would have likely gotten me to understand this circular dynamic.

Being in the presence of those who are near the end of their physical world journey and learning from them, gives one a new perspective and inspires new questions:

How does compassion for patients lead me to feel compassion for myself?

Will that in turn lead to forgiveness?

Is there a mysterious spiritual element that greases the wheel of the volunteer-client relationship and leads to a type of healing for one or both?

How is it that I am learning how to heal from those who cannot heal?

I love the questions. One may never completely heal from some wounds, but we can learn to carry them differently. As author Anthony Goulet has written, "Count your scars as the number of times you've been healed, not wounded."[1] Thank God for my scars.

Epilogue

In the process of writing *The Music Between Us,* I discovered some of my mother's history, previously unknown to me. On January 27, 1936, Sofia Mendelsohn Berkowitz, my maternal grandmother, lost her footing while descending a building stoop in New York City, on Manhattan's Lower East Side. She may have been distracted by my four-year-old mother, the youngest of her three children, who was with her. Eight months pregnant, Sophia stumbled to the pavement and landed on her stomach. Just thirty-six years old, she died four days later from a ruptured uterus. The baby she carried also did not survive.

On March 13, just six weeks later, my mother, along with her two older siblings, was placed into foster care. She had lost her mother, an unborn sibling, and was separated from her father, all before turning five years old. She and her siblings wound up living in a succession of homes because my grandfather couldn't take care of them.

In 1942, at age ten, my mother was reunited with her older brother, sister, and their father. Three months later, he enlisted in the Army, abandoning her once again.

There is an unpredictable interplay of genetics and environment that tilts one towards schizoaffective disorder. Even if my mother had not been genetically predisposed to schizophrenia or bipolar, the childhood traumas she suffered might very well have left her with disabling emotional scars impacting her for the rest of her life.

Did my mother believe, on some level, that she caused the deaths of her own mother and unborn sibling in the accident? Was her separation and abandonment by her father seen by her young brain as punishment for the breakup of her family?

Several factors are presumed to be related to the severity of schizoaffective disorder in an individual. These might include free will, self-awareness, and intelligence. Although their influence, for better or for worse, is immeasurable, each contributes in some way to the person's ability to manage their symptoms. Unfortunately, these qualities, which we all possess in varying degrees, did not seem to combine in a manner that was to my mother's advantage.

My mother died in her sleep at age seventy-six. She left an envelope with some cash behind, but no other possessions of particular importance aside from three wallet-sized grade school pictures in her purse—one of each of her three grade-school-aged sons.

Acknowledgments

It can be a challenge to understand how every significant relationship you have ever had has influenced who you are and what you are becoming. Everyone leaves their mark in some way. As a memoir, this book is partly a tribute to valuable family, friends, teachers, professional colleagues, and spiritual guides. Each has influenced me in some mysterious way that indirectly led to the creation of *The Music Between Us.* I hope you know who you are. As one might expect, there are many people to thank for their direct support and assistance in the creation of this book.

I dedicate *The Music Between Us* to my family and especially my spouse, Cynthia, both for her enthusiasm and encouragement for my writing and, most of all, for her commitment to the life we created together. I also appreciate her for gently correcting my memories of that life as expressed in the book. Also, I am grateful to my daughters, Ariel and Stephanie, who have loved me in spite of my flaws; and to my brothers, Mitch and Stu, for sharing their memories of our parents and helping me verify my own recollections.

Thank you to my friend Rania Anderson for giving me the idea to write a book. A successful author in her own right, Rania suggested how I might weave the stories of my client interactions within a bigger story of personal transformation.

She has been with me every step of the way, advising, critiquing, and otherwise being helpful with many aspects of this project. Thanks also to Rania's husband, my close friend Lance for his ideas and support.

A grateful thanks to my cousin Karyn Gold, whom I barely knew before undertaking this book. She generously shared her childhood memories and provided documented history of family members that I had not known existed.

Thanks to Crossroads Hospice and Ascend Hospice for their outstanding commitment to patients and their families as well as to volunteers like me. Special gratitude to Barbara Poe and Josh Braman, the hospice volunteer professionals who have matched me and my style of music with people who might best benefit from a bedside visit. Both supported the writing of the book and read the earliest version of the manuscript. Their feedback gently shaped my perception of hospice volunteering. They also pushed me to clearly express how the dynamic between myself and clients revealed new memories and led to observations about my life.

Thank you to my professional mentor, Sonia Farrand, a media sales industry leader. She spent years coaching me out of some of the bad habits and behaviors I displayed when interacting with colleagues and business customers, knowing how important that would be for my career and for me personally. Thanks also to Jim Doyle, a person who models the power of volunteerism, having spent much of his life regularly working with people who have various needs.

Thank you to my dear friends Mike Eggleston, Jim Carmody, and Jim Weinstein, the men of my weekly spiritual support group. Over the course of three years, they listened patiently as I described my journey and helped me to view my memoir within a spiritual context.

Thanks to all the authors who inspired me with writings that have deeply explored some of the themes in the book. Among them: Mitch Albom (*Tuesdays With Morrie*), Wally Lamb (*I Know This Much is True*), David Brooks (*The Second Mountain*), Richard Rohr (*Falling Upward*), and anything written by Anne Lamott or Kathleen Norris.

Thank you to Stephanie Gunning, my talented editor and publishing consultant. She provided expert advice on shaping the story and bringing it to life while walking me through the publishing process. Her knowledge and encouragement have been priceless. I would also like to acknowledge Gus Yoo for his cover design, Lorena Raven for her guitar doodle, and Najat Washington for her work in preparing the book's interior layout.

Thanks to Claude Brunell, Ph.D., and Masooma Sheikh, M.D., who each have extensive experience treating patients with schizophrenia and their families. They each shaped and clarified my understanding and descriptions of the disorder. Most importantly, they helped me to understand how it may have impacted me throughout my life as well as others in similar family situations.

Thank you to Father Ed Sheridan, who was the parish priest at Saint Gabriel Catholic Church when I lived in Charlotte, North Carolina. He imaginatively used his impressive knowledge of Judaism to provide compelling reasons not to leave the faith of my birth before succumbing to my wishes and guiding my conversion to Christianity.

Thanks to the book's advance reader team for reviewing the first draft of the manuscript and sharing what worked and what did not, from the quality of the writing to the story themes: Nancy Dupre Barnes, Rigby Barnes, Marcia Bergren, Reverend Amanda Goin-Burgess, Karmel Carothers, MD., Reverend Trish Nelson, Stephanie Wildman, and Dave Raney.

Thanks to a few fingerstyle acoustic guitarists from whom I have learned much of what I play. Special gratitude to my good friend Australian master fingerstyle player Nick Charles who continues to generously coach my playing technique and teach me many of the songs we think my clients might like. Thanks also to musicians, both living and gone, David Hamburger, Ed Gerhard, Lance Anderson, Tommy Emmanuel, Stephan Grossman, Lonnie Johnson, and Mississippi John Hurt, for their influence on my playing and their lifetime of contributions to the enjoyment of guitar music. They each lifted my expectations for myself as a musician.

And finally, my deepest gratitude to the hundreds of clients and their families who accept me into their space, allowing me to participate as they approach the next leg of their journey.

Credits

Epigraphs to the Book

Lao Tzu was a sixth century B.C.E. Chinese philosopher, known as the author of *Tao Te Ching.*

Dick Clark. "Q&A with Dick Clark," *Los Angeles Times* (February 7, 1994).

Philip Yancey. *What's So Amazing about Grace?* (Grand Rapids, MI.: Zondervan, 1997).

Preface

Aldous Huxley. *Music at Night: And Other Essays* (London, U.K.: Chatto & Windus, 1931).

Introduction

The epigraph has often been attributed to Plato, although, as far as I can tell, it does not appear in any of his works.

Chapter One

Boudleaux Bryant, "All I Have to Do Is Dream," 1958.

Chapter Two

Alex North and Hy Zaret, "Unchained Melody," 1955.

Chapter Three

Epigraph: Frederick Delius (1862–1934) was a British composer of orchestral music and opera.

Chapter Five

Epigraph: Vera Nazarian (born 1966) is an American fantasy and science fiction writer.

Chapter Six

Epigraph. Hans Christian Anderson, Danish author (1805–1875).

Chapter Seven

Epigraph: Confucius (551–479 B.C.E.) was a Chinese philosopher who valued morality, kindness, justice, and sincerity.

Chapter Eight

Epigraph: "I Feel Like I'm Fixin' to Die Rag," words and music by Joe McDonald © 1965 renewed 1993 by Alkatraz Corner Music Co. Used by permission.

Chapter Nine

Epigraph: Plato. *The Republic* (360 B.C.E.), translated by Benjamin Jowett.

Chapter Ten

Epigraph: Attributed to W.B. Stevens, alternate Barney E. Warren. "Farther Along" (1911).

Chapter Eleven

Epigraph: Leonard Bernstein. *The Unanswered Question: Six Talks at Harvard* (Cambridge, MA.: Harvard University Press, 1976), p. 140.

1. Valerie Strauss. "When a First-grader's Wrong Answer Was Better than the Right One," *Washington Post* (January 3, 2018).

Chapter Twelve

Epigraph: Anna Akhmatova, excerpt from "March Elegies" from *Complete Poems of Anna Akhmatova*, translated by Judith Hemschemeyer, edited and introduced by Roberta Reeder. Copyright © 1989, 1992, 1997 by Judith Hemschemeyer. Reprinted with the permission of The Permissions Company, LLC on behalf of Zephyr Press, zephyrpress.org, and by Canongate Books, Canongate.co.uk.

Chapter Thirteen

Epigraph: William Shakespeare. *Twelfth Night,* Act I, Scene 1.

Chapter Fourteen

Epigraph: Frank Zappa and Peter Occhiogrosso. *The Real Frank Zappa Book* (New York: Touchstone, 1989), p. 193.

Chapter Fifteen

Epigraph: Edward Bulwer-Lytton. *Zanoni* (1856).

Chapter Sixteen

Epigraph: Arthur "Blind" Blake. "Chump Man Blues," recorded by Paramount Records, 1929.

Chapter Seventeen
Epigraph: Robert (Bobby) Troup. "(Get Your Kicks on) Route 66." Released as a single by Capitol Records, 1946. Reprinted by permission of Hal Leonard.

Chapter Eighteen
Epigraph: Leopold Stokowski. Taken from an address to an audience at Carnegie Hall, as quoted in *New York Times* (May 11, 1967).

Chapter Nineteen
Epigraph: Walter Donaldson and Gus Kahn, "Makin' Whoopee," 1928.

Chapter Twenty
Epigraph: Kurt Vonnegut. Twitter post (July 6, 2012), https://twitter.com/kurt_vonnegut/status/221363080913883136?lang=en.

Chapter Twenty-One
Epigraph: Bettina von Arnim in a letter to Johann Wolfgang von Goethe dated May 28, 1810. From *Goethe's Briefwechsel mit einem Kinde: Seinem Denkmal, Volume 2* (Dümmler, 1835), p. 193.

Chapter Twenty-Two
Epigraph: Jerry Leiber, Mike Stoller, and Ben E. King. "Stand by Me," *Don't Play That Song!* Single released by Atco Records, 1961. Reprinted by permission of Hal Leonard.

Chapter Twenty-Three

Epigraph: Wolfgang Amadeus Mozart was a composer (1756–1791).

Chapter Twenty-Four

Paul Simon. "Graceland," *Graceland.* Released by Universal Music Publishing Group. 1986. Reprinted by permission of Hal Leonard.

1. Sam Philip. "Rock's Visionary," Sun Record Company website (accessed May 25, 2020), http://www.sunrecord company.com/Sam_Phillips.html.

Chapter Twenty-Five

Epigraph: Jerry Leiber and Mike Stoller, "Kansas City," 1952. Reprinted by permission of Hal Leonard.

1. Robert Johnson, "Sweet Home Chicago," 1937. Reprinted by permission of Hal Leonard.

Chapter Twenty-Six

Epigraph: Reverend Augustus Toplady, "Rock of Ages," 1763

Chapter Twenty-Seven

Epigraph: James M. Barrie. *Peter Pan* (the play), 1954.

1. Matthew 6:25. The Holy Bible, English Standard Version. ESV® Text Edition: 2016. Copyright © 2001 by Crossway Bibles, a publishing ministry of Good News Publishers.

Chapter Twenty-Eight

Epigraph: Laurence Vittes. "Exclusive Interview with Yo Yo Ma on the Spirituality of Music," HuffPost (September 30, 2012).

Chapter Twenty-Nine
Epigraph: Carlos Santana. Class Trailer. "Carlos Santana Teaches the
Art and Soul of Guitar," MasterClass (accessed May 23, 2020).

Chapter Thirty
Epigraph: Johann Wolfgang von Goethe was a writer and statesman (1749–1832). "Chapter 1," *Wilhelm Meister's Apprenticeship, Volume 5* (Berlin: Johann Friedrich Unger, 1795–1796).

Chapter Thirty-One
Epigraph: Joan Walsh Anglund. *A Cup of Sun: A Book of Poems* (New York: Harcourt, 1967), p. 15.

Chapter Thirty-Two
Epigraph: Percy Bysshe Shelley. "Music, When Soft Voices Die" *Posthumous Poems* (London, England: John and Henry L. Hunt, 1824).

Chapter Thirty-Three
Epigraph: Thomas Carlyle. *Critical & Miscellaneous Essays: Collected & Republished* (1857).
1. Anthony Goulet. "Count Your Scars as the Number of Times You've Been Healed, Not Wounded," Good Men Project (September 13, 2014).

Resources

Thank you for reading my book.

There are a number of themes that continuously intersect throughout my story. Among them: a bit of contemporary music history, music and the brain, coping with mental illness in one's family, recognizing the signs of a spiritual awakening in one's life, and, of course, the mystery of how one may come fully alive to one's true self while serving others.

It is my hope that if you are interested in knowing more about any of the book's themes, you have a place to start. If you or anyone you know wants to know more, please visit my website, www.stevelitwer.com, and subscribe to the blog. There you'll also find links to Spotify playlists featuring different genres of music, including the complete set of songs from this book.

Periodically new resources will be added to the website, including news of upcoming events and featured artists.

Hear Steve play on his YouTube channel; search for "Steve Litwer."

Follow Steve on Facebook at "Steve Litwer, Author."

Link to Steve on LinkedIn at:
https://www.linkedin.com/in/steve-litwer-0507066.

To request an interview with the author, schedule a speaking engagement, or place a bulk book order, please send an email to info@stevelitwer.com.

ABOUT THE AUTHOR

Steve Litwer lives in Overland Park, Kansas, a suburb of Kansas City. He plays guitar for dying people in hospice care and their families. He grew up in New York and New Jersey and attended Emporia State University and the University of Kansas. He is a retired media sales executive, having spent his career in advertising sales management for radio, broadcast TV, and cable TV. Married to Cynthia Litwer, he is the father of two children and a grandfather. He lives and makes music in the Kansas City metropolitan area. *The Music Between Us* is his first book.